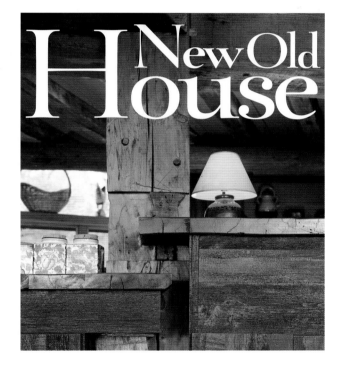

H New Old ouse

Ed Knapp

H New Old ouse

Designing with Reclaimed Materials

Gibbs Smith, Publisher
Salt Lake City

First Paperback Edition
09 08 07 06 05   5 4 3 2 1

Published by
Gibbs Smith, Publisher
P.O. Box 667
Layton, Utah 840401

Orders: (1-800) 835-4993
www.gibbs-smith.com

Project directed by Suzanne Gibbs Taylor
Edited by Elissa Altman
Designed and produced by Kurt Wahlner
Printed in China

Library of Congress Cataloging-in-Publication Data

Knapp, Ed
  New Old House : designing with reclaimed materials / Ed Knapp.—
1st ed.
    p. cm.
   ISBN 1-58685-049-0 (hb); 1-58685-842-4 (pbk)
  1. Antiques in interior decoration. 2. Found objects (Art) in
interior decoration. I. Title.
  NK2115.5.A 5 .K59 2002
  747—dc21
                            2002005189

WALNUT

OAK

POPLAR

Acknowledgements

My deep thanks go to all the people and customers through the years who have purchased or been involved with the recycling process of our structures. Without their interest, I would not have written this book. I would also like to thank all the people and companies who have participated in our demolition and salvage operations. May you all live well and be safe.

To my many friends and past and present co-workers: thank you for all of your hard work. There is a special bond between us—you know who you are!

To Suzanne Taylor, my editor, for her interest and belief in me to complete this project. I have enjoyed and grown with each page.

A special thanks to my family—my children, my wife Spring, and my parents Elaine and Bill—for all their patience and support through the years. I especially want to thank my mother for her work and support on this book. I would also like to thank Judy Paine for all her special help.

And finally, to all of you out there who cherish the beauty of reclaimed materials and share the dream of incorporating them into contemporary design.

C O N T E N T S

Introduction

Grover Cleveland was between presidential terms when the barn on my grandparents' farm was built outside Buffalo, New York, in 1882. The deed for the farm itself appears in public records as far back as the early 1700s, when it was owned by the Holland Land Company, one of the earliest Dutch settlement organizations in what we now refer to as the New World. The barn had a stable with stanchions for milk cows, two-horse stalls, and a hayloft over the stable. This part of the building was warm even during the coldest western New York winters, when the snow that Buffalo is so famous for piled up in drifts between the house and the other outbuildings. The rest of the huge windowless interior was used for hay and feed storage as well as a place to keep the farm equipment, and was usually bitter cold in the dead of winter. Years after it was built, this weathered, utilitarian, *beautiful* outbuilding became a very special place for grandchildren (including me) to swing on a rope from one of the high, massive hand-hewn beams, and drop safely into the fresh hay piled below it.

Time went by and many things in my young life changed, as they invariably do. But my grandparents' barn has always had a unique and lasting place in my heart; it *was* history—both mine and theirs. Buffalo winters came and went, children and grandchildren grew up, many years passed and our nation saw two world wars, but the barn remained steadfast as a functional working piece of history, owing much of its survival and beauty to the simple reliability and strength of its craftsmanship.

As I became more involved in building with wood, I began to place high value on the integrity and *love of craft* that was exemplified in the building of old barns, and it became apparent to me that there was a strong need for these very concepts to be utilized in our overly modernized lives, especially in our homes. I dedicated myself to developing ways in which I could put these concepts of craftsmanship, history, and integrity of design into practice. As I saw many grand old barns starting to fall into disrepair, neglected because of the lack of interest in saving them or available funds to maintain them, I lamented the enormous waste of resources. Yet, simultaneously, I considered how materials

"Years after it was built, this weathered, utilitarian, beautiful outbuilding became a very special place for grandchildren (including me) to swing on a rope from one of the high, massive hand-hewn beams, and drop safely into the fresh hay piled below." Photo courtesy of Sally Bowen Travis.

such as old barn wood might be reused in other buildings, applying the same concepts of craftsmanship, quality, and integrity employed in historical building methods.

After much research and a vain attempt to find books or resources that might teach me the best way to go about such a potentially overwhelming project, I simply started on my own, documenting historical building procedures as I went along. I made many mistakes in buying and using these old materials, and though many of my friends and family could not understand why anyone would want to invest in this type of construction, there were also many people along the way who helped enlighten me by sharing their ideas.

Eventually, I founded Vintage Beams & Timbers, Inc., which is based in Barkers Creek Valley in the Smoky Mountains of western North Carolina; the Pisgah National Forest, where the U.S. Forest Service began and is now based, is just down the road. Vintage Beams is dedicated to preserving antique lumber and timber through its use in many applications, including creative design. Antique timbers are pressure-washed to enhance their various golden tones, then cleaned, fumigated, and stored in preparation for ongoing projects. Our yard is filled with a variety of mantels, barn board, heart-pine, teak flooring, rough-sawn wood, beams, old tin, and—since we are an international import-export company—antique bricks and unique hand-carved pieces from China. The creative possibilities in using reclaimed materials are endless: an old cabin can be purchased and placed on a special property, or

Photo by Susie Adams.

one can be custom-built from beautiful old logs. Folks are always encouraged to stop by for a visit and discuss the use of salvaged materials and hard-to-find old timber that we've brought here from around the world.

As we face the next hundred years, what are we going to leave behind in our architecture, our homes, and our way of life? Will it be strip malls, or prefabricated, poorly built homes designed with a life span of ten to twenty years? Hopefully, there will be a balance of homes passed on for the future, with definite character, beauty, and a depth of quality in timber, design integrity, and craftsmanship. I'm optimistic that, a century or two from now, someone will look at what we've created and say, "What can we save out of this? What can we reclaim, and reuse?" It is my hope that we will hand off a baton of legacies from the last two hundred years, to be used again and again, to be appreciated, learned from, lived with, and cherished, like my grandparents' barn.

Ed Knapp
2002

Photo by Gil Stose.

11

The Legacy of Reclaimed Materials

Look around you. What do you see being wasted in an old structure in the country, or even in the city? What materials are being discarded? Are you able to see beyond the dust, the chipping paint, or the mortise holes to the underlying craftsmanship, the *legacy* that discarded materials may hold, and the historical stories they can tell? What can you do with it? What can you design with it? How can it become a physical, *living* part of your home? What are *you* wasting? What can you yourself pass on in a society that already has so much?

In the twenty-first century, recycling has become a regular part of our lives: we sort used materials into that which can be reused, and that which can't. Under nearly every desk in every corporation, both major and minor, are two trash cans—one for recyclables and one for non-recyclables. There are even environmentally aware companies such as Yvon Chounard's Patagonia and Malden Mills that create warm, functional, beautiful clothing from the most unlikely resources: used plastic soda bottles.

But recycling isn't limited to the wastepaper basket or the garbage bin: all over the country, in rural areas as well as in bustling cities, antiques shops stand side by side with chain stores; collectors and average shoppers alike spend hours looking for a diamond in the rough, that special

Photo by Gil Stose.

Recycled copper piping does new duty as an eye-catching way to hang pots and other cookware, as in the kitchen of this North Carolina mountain home. The combination of gleaming copper and stainless-steel pans provides a visual respite from the other construction materials used in the house, including unpolished stone and reclaimed wood. Photo by Susie Adams.

An antique fishing creel can be used as a rustic way to display fresh-cut flowers anywhere there's a peg or a hook. Photo by Susie Adams.

something for their homes that was discarded long ago. It might be a long-closed post office's solid oak mail sorter, now doing creative service somewhere as a spice holder or a compact disc stand. An old discarded oak filing cabinet may find new life as a built-in storage space for treasured record albums. Or it might be something, perhaps, with an engraved insignia that offers a clue—and a link—to the item's history.

Antiques, whatever they are and however we use them, are often well-crafted, well-designed connections to the past. Reclaimed, salvaged antique wood and other traditional construction materials are no different.

Reclaiming Construction Materials

Beyond its purely aesthetic potential, the concept of *reclaiming materials* is alive and well in all of its various guises, and is an important way for us to preserve our limited resources, particularly wood. While forests are a renewable resource, they are certainly not renewed quickly. And as our building and logging boom continues, we must keep in mind that, in the United States, construction materials *alone* comprise approximately 60 percent of our landfill burden. The use of reclaimed construction materials—old barn wood, flooring, beams, and much more—is a highly practical way to preserve our natural resources. And hand in hand with practicality go the issues of quality, design integrity, and craftsmanship that enable a musty load of nineteenth-century, hand-planed pine flooring to be pressure-cleaned to its original beauty and reused today, many generations later. In most cases, the design integrity and quality that enabled its survival is incomparable.

> Antiques are often well-crafted, well-designed connections to the past. Reclaimed traditional construction materials are no different.

Production and design of construction materials has come a long way since the days of hand-carving individual beams and boards for a home or a barn. A process that used to take days and even weeks has been transformed into an industry standard: uniform building materials are created by forming the wood with motorized sawmills and modern milling machines. Production times are swift, but the quality is low and the craftsmanship next to nonexistent. The character of the materials—the grain pattern, life, history, and functionality: that which makes wood *wood*—becomes of secondary importance as they are being quick-formed and machine-milled for immediate use. Compare a modern 2 x 6-foot board from your local lumberyard to an old pit-sawn board of similar dimensions. There is simply no comparison in quality or character.

Designing with Reclaimed Materials

Aside from the obvious conservation and historical implications that come with the use of reclaimed (or salvaged) building materials is the issue of aesthetics: a wide range of these materials is providing an entirely new perspective in home design. From down home to downtown, salvaged materials are showing up in state-of-the-art country kitchens as cabinetry; as sharply contrasting, distressed flooring and detailing in otherwise monochromatic modern living lofts; and, more simply, in the re-creation of traditional-style homes whose owners long for the authenticity, practicality, and craftsmanship of these beautiful materials.

When an old weathered barn comes down either because it has literally caved in after generations of use, or is taken down because it has fallen into disrepair and is a liability to the farmer, its wood is still decidedly stronger, more durable, and probably more beautiful than any of its modern counterparts. Old barn wood is hand-hewn, well-crafted, and very strong—neither its properties nor its history can be duplicated using today's resources and methods. Reusing this wood means a second life for this fine material. It also means maintaining a direct connection with the wood's history. The expectation is that its legacy of craftsmanship and design integrity will be carried into future generations.

In many cases, entire buildings that have been demolished are being reclaimed by architectural salvage companies, moved, and then rebuilt from scratch as new/old buildings; their interiors, replete with modern conveniences, are perfectly juxtaposed against the rich, aged craftsmanship of the original building's materials.

In response to this call for reclaimed materials, recycling and architectural salvage companies that handle a range of materials are springing up all over the country. It is evident that there is a vital need to educate homeowners, homebuilders, architects, and designers in using recycled wood and other building materials by implementing the traditional applications and techniques that have enabled the materials to survive in the first place. *New Old House* will educate, offer suggestions, address problems *before* they crop up, and ultimately showcase the myriad design possibilities and creative applications associated with utilizing antique recycled materials, while maintaining the ages-old traditions on which they were originally built.

Vintage Beams & Timbers draws no lines at the creative reuse of discarded everyday materials: these rattraps keep a firm grip on employee paychecks and other important messages. And yes, the killer springs have been removed. Photo by Susie Adams.

An antique Ferris wheel seat finds a new life after being creatively converted to a porch swing.
Photo by Susie Adams.

Dark granite countertops, an island sink, and soft high-hat lighting are some of the modern amenities that easily work hand in hand with reclaimed antique cabinetry and flooring in this modern country kitchen.
Photo by Gil Stose.

Joe and Bette CARRIER and Family

Early in the 1980s, Joe Carrier's gambrel barn in Cuba, New York, was in very poor shape; one whole end was blown down. In those days, it was really an adventure to walk up to a stranger's farmhouse, knock on the door, and say, "Hi, I'm Ed Knapp, and I'm interested in taking down your barn." At that time, the industry was fairly new, and people had not generally accepted that there was a market for this type of architectural design product.

When I happened upon Joe Carrier, he was interested in what I had to say, and he invited me in. He showed me through his barn and told me the history of his family. His great-great-grandfather had built the structure in 1901, and the farm had been occupied by the family ever since that time. Together, they lived and worked with a high standard of integrity, and the barn reflected those ideals. As I got to know Joe better, I sensed he would be relieved to have someone who cared dismantle the dilapidated structure, and pass it on to another generation.

We discussed the logistics of taking down the building, cleaning up the site, and detailing what would remain. He wanted to keep the barn foundation and also the thick concrete slab where the milk house had been located. We eventually got down to what I would be willing to pay him for the old barn—$850 for the job. Negotiations were ended with a handshake, and a small contract was written so that in the event of unforeseen circumstances,

Photo courtesy of the Carrier family.

An Old Soul
Goes to a New Home

Shown as it stood before dismantling, the Carrier barn was a total liability and the family was very happy to find a new use for the old timber. Photo by Ed Knapp.

everyone would know what was in the original agreement.

The project progressed very well. There were some problems bringing the barn down because the equipment we used did not reach far enough, so a lot of wood was damaged. Nearly 40 percent of the wood was lost, but we managed to save the timbers.

At the same time, I was constructing and helping design a new home in Highlands, North Carolina. The owner was very involved in the project and had a great interest in Joe Carrier, the history of the barn, and the process of taking it down. The family decided that they wanted the beams from Joe's barn for their new house.

Eventually, the barn beams and boards were loaded onto tractor-trailer trucks, and were ready to start the trip south to my company's home in western North Carolina,

The Carrier barn had generations of use before being reclaimed. Shown here from left to right are Joe's great-great-grandfather, Philo Carrier, grandfather, Joseph Philo Carrier, and father, Clifford Vance Carrier. Photos courtesy of the Carrier family.

and then to the construction site. I took a picture for Joe and gave it to him as a record of the barn. After I paid him, we sat down with an old family album and other books that showed pictures of the barn being built and how it grew.

Joe talked about his great-great-grandfather, Philo Carrier, who was born in the house in 1805 before it had windows and doors in place to keep the weather out; he spoke of his grandfather, Joseph Philo Carrier, who worked in Olean, New York, hauling milk in milk cans and laboring in railroad car shops during the Great Depression; and he talked about his father, Clifford Vance Carrier, who worked in the oil fields in the Olean area, and drove trucks to Buffalo, New York. The Carrier family moved back into the house on the farm when Joe was four years old.

Originally, he told me, the barn was built as a dairy barn; it was 40 by 80 feet and three stories high. It contained two horse stalls, some box stalls, and enough room to milk 30 to 35 cows. A large structure was needed to protect the stock in the winter, as the average yearly snowfall was 80 inches. The dairy business continued until 1968.

In the days when the barn was built, the material for building came from the local lumber company. The skilled craftsmen, timberwrights, and carpenters bought the package, which included the windows, doors, and nails. When it came time for the barn to be

erected, the owner was responsible for gathering together as many neighbors, relatives, and friends as possible, along with their horses and mules, to help "raise the barn" in a day. This is still done today, especially by the Amish.

As Joe and I went through the old materials list still kept by his family, we saw the prices of wood, nails, roofing, windows, doors, hinges, and labor; it came to a total of $843, seven dollars short of the amount that I paid him for the barn many years later.

Joe and his wife Bette were very pleased that their barn had found a new home in the Highlands Mountain property in North Carolina. The Carriers came to see the house as it was being built, and could actually remember the timbers and where they had been placed in the barn. They reminisced about the story of the cherry tree that had to be cut down at the last minute when the barn was being built because it was one timber short. Today, that same beam has a prominent place of honor in its new living room.

Part of the Carrier family history is now in a new location, and will be protected and admired for years to come. This is a much better solution emotionally and economically for antique wood than to see it in a big burn pile.

I would like to dedicate this chapter to Joe and Bette Carrier's family—past, present and future—as it reflects the generations of families and craftsmen whose work has been carried into the twenty-first century.

The Carriers were ultimately very pleased to see their barn reborn in a newly designed home in North Carolina, which blends the rough-hewn timbers of the Carrier barn with modern elegance. Photo by Ed Knapp.

The Hidden Beauty of Reclaimed Materials

When you first set foot in a renovated kitchen or in a new home with spectacular mountain views and lovely furniture, what draws your attention? It might be a glistening, stainless-steel commercial range, or perhaps the handmade kilim pillows on a Mission-style sofa in front of a picture window. But more than likely, and much more subtly, you will be immediately drawn to the warmth, depth, and craftsmanship of the reclaimed cherry kitchen cabinetry, or the way the salvaged teak floors and the hand-hewn antique beams brought in by a recycling company practically envelop you. Wood—once a living substance—possesses an almost magnetic quality unequalled by any other construction material. But salvaged wood, as well as other reclaimed construction materials, doesn't generally start out as beautiful to the untrained eye. As a matter of fact, the panic that ensues when untrained homeowners take delivery of a pile of dirty, dusty, reclaimed construction materials is usually followed by a series of unprintable expletives, which is further followed by a resounding "WHAT are we going to do with THIS?"

Over the course of my life of working with reclaimed wood, I have encountered many instances of what I now refer to as "old-timber wood shock." When wood is seen as an intrinsic part of an existing barn or is built into a home, its beauty is obvious: there is instant admiration

for the quality and the look of its antique richness. However, when the wood is taken from a preexisting structure, loaded onto a truck, and delivered to a new construction site, all that can be seen by the untrained eye is a large pile of nondescript dirty old wood. Likewise, when an *entire* antique structure has been taken down and transported elsewhere for rebuilding, it looks like an unimaginable, uninhabitable mess.

This is a very difficult phase for most homeowners—and many builders—because they simply cannot envision the old wood being integrated into a new or existing design; nor can they visualize how it will enhance the total project. To make matters worse, this pile of wood, brick, or timbers has probably cost a considerable amount of money. Furthermore, the panic can be fueled by neighbors, friends, spouses—even carpenters—who will invariably comment, "What have you done now?" and "I wouldn't put this stuff in my chicken coop!" or "Honey, we spent HOW much for this stuff? What are we going to do with it? Can this old wood possibly look like anything but *old wood?*"

My response is always the same: "Relax. It's going to be okay. Remember what you have seen in pictures and what I showed you in completed projects. Keep in mind what your original ideas were, and I will walk you through the process of making the materials beautiful again."

> When wood is taken from a preexisting structure and delivered to a construction site, all that can be seen by the untrained eye is a pile of nondescript dirty old wood.

This modernized kitchen is a wonderful example of the use of highly distressed, reclaimed wood cabinetry and beams. Note the far wall behind the cook top; peg holes, knotting, a tenon slot, and the pure textural roughness of the materials work together to create an enormously real, warm, yet modern environment. Photo by Gil Stose.

When endeavoring to work with reclaimed materials, it's an absolute necessity to be able to look beyond the "big, ugly pile of wood" that will invariably arrive at your job site. If you look closely at these beams, you can see tenon slots, peg holes, chinking, and other indications of high design integrity. Barn wood is extremely stable and will provide a vast amount of usable reclaimed materials. Notice the tagging at the end of the reclaimed beam. Photos by Ed Knapp.

Photo by Ed Knapp.

Photo by Susie Adams.

A Desire to Live with Historical Craftsmanship

As a homeowner, architect, builder, or designer, you have already made the initial leap by simply *wanting* to integrate reclaimed materials into your home or project, for historical, conservational, practical, or purely aesthetic purposes (or a combination of all of the above); and so, after the initial "timber shock" wears off, you will easily get beyond the panic stage. Frankly, there is nothing that can duplicate the design integrity, craftsmanship, and quality of reclaimed materials. Somewhere, deep inside, even as you stand looking (and worrying) over a load of dirty materials, you *know* this (otherwise, you wouldn't be reading this book). That said, the salvage company with whom you are working should take the time to explain exactly *what* you are looking at, what the cleaning and restoring process will entail, and how it will change the visual nature of the reclaimed materials, because it will.

Also, reclaimed wood very often does not possess the same functional qualities as new wood: it's usually not as flexible as new wood, and that may affect how and where you plan to use it, generally for the better. Again, the professional you work with will explain this to you, address any specific concerns that you have, and try to set your mind at ease.

Knowing for sure that the reclaimed wood you have purchased is fit for construction or rebuilding is of obvious and extreme importance. Some of the most common questions I'm asked about antique wood are "It's old, but will it be okay?" and "Is it any good? Wouldn't new wood be better structurally?" The answers to those questions are "yes, yes, and no." The strength of the old growth from which the wood comes, along with its outstanding physical density, makes it absolutely ideal for use in modern applications.

Old wood will not flex as far as new-growth material, which, in construction, is of prime importance, since the denser the wood is and the less flex it has, the more secure and stable it will be. Additionally, if the older wood has been kept dry, it will be even *more* stable.

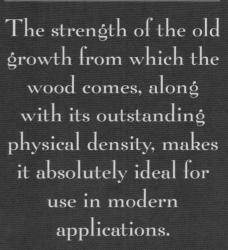

When reclaimed timber is brought to Vintage Beams & Timbers, an important part of the process it goes through is pressure-washing. Here, reclaimed timbers are put through this process to remove years of built-up detritus, dust, and dirt. The result will be a clean but weathered look.

> The strength of the old growth from which the wood comes, along with its outstanding physical density, makes it absolutely ideal for use in modern applications.

The Effects of Moisture

The moisture content of old wood can have a powerful effect on flooring, paneling, and timber, but not for the best. When wood is dry, say at 8 percent moisture content, it is very stable. If that wood absorbs moisture from rain, or from improper protection or covering, the moisture content goes up to a whopping 20 or 25 percent, which means the wood is extremely wet. If wet wood is put into a home or building and has not been allowed to lose some moisture—or to stabilize—it will expand to a larger size and weight as it dries. About six months after this wet material is installed, it will begin to dry out, returning to its original 8-percent moisture content. As this occurs, there will be a tremendous amount of gapping, checking, and spacing between the adjoining materials, which will then become a major structural problem for everyone concerned: the homeowner, the builder, and the wood supplier.

A Word to the Professional

Wood that is registering 8 percent moisture content on a moisture meter may absorb additional moisture while in transit to the job site. If at all possible, store it inside the structure it's meant for, and allow about ten days to three weeks for the wood to acclimate. This will vary greatly in different parts of the country. For example, the moisture content in a house on the beach in Florida will certainly have a much higher moisture-content rating than a similar structure in the Arizona desert, where the rating might be about 3 percent. When the wood has been allowed to acclimate and stabilize, there will be very little movement after installation because the moisture content will have become equal to that of the surrounding environment.

The stability and strength of these beams are simply unmatched; the wood is very old, very dry, and very strong. Photo by Susie Adams.

New wood and wet wood—especially that which is used in *timberwright* (the method of using heavy timber for structural post-and-beam applications)—will move, check, and crack if used in construction. As the timber begins to "cure," it can move in different ways, crack glass, push walls, and cause other severely damaging and potentially dangerous structural problems. It can take up to two or three years to cure large, freshly sawn logs to be used as beams. Using antique lumber—timber that has been cured and dried in a structure for more than one hundred years—can eliminate the process of waiting and wondering (and worrying) about stability.

> Using antique lumber— timber that has been cured and dried in a structure for more than one hundred years—can eliminate the process of waiting and wondering (and worrying) about stability.

Moreover, if you are a professional and are examining the wood yourself, you can pick and choose the pieces that have clearly remained very solid and straight. When a green tree is cut and sawn into a beam, it has, as we have noted, a tendency to move to some degree in the direction that it naturally grows. With old timbers, the wood has "already made the move," as the saying goes. Reclaimed timbers that were cured eons ago, however, will not move; hence, the stability factor that makes this antique material so desired in post-and-beam construction.

Design Considerations: Color, Characteristics, and Personal Taste

As a homeowner who has made the decision to either utilize reclaimed materials in your home or to have an entire salvaged structure (a dilapidated barn, for example) rebuilt on your property, you most likely have done so for a combination of reasons: Raw, hand-hewn beauty. Unmatched physical stability. History. Practicality. But what about the issues of personal taste—*your* personal taste? Of style and color? Once the materials are cleaned, fumigated, pressure-washed and ready to become part of your home (or possibly, your entire home), how will *you* live with them?

The astounding beauty of restored hand-hewn materials is obvious; they both subtly and dramatically draw attention to themselves. They speak of magnificent craftsman-

The Physical Qualities of Antique Timber

One of the most common reasons for using antique timber and wood is, among other things, its wonderful physical qualities. In most cases, antique wood and timber was cut from "old growth" virgin forests, which means that the trees were several hundred years old or older. Old-growth forests are those in which trees have grown in active competition for moisture and sunlight. The stunning quality of these stately old trees results in a much more tightly grained material; the tighter the growth rings, the better quality the timber. (Likewise, the more you move inward from the outer layers of the tree where the limbs grow, the greater the chance that the material is clear of "knots.") It is this stability that makes old-growth wood so much more valuable than new wood, enabling it to survive for so long in use. Old-growth wood tends to also be prized for its maturity, its beauty, and the many different colors it takes on during the aging process.

ship, of the kind of design integrity and quality that most artisans today can only attempt to emulate. So is it appropriate to discuss color matching? Is it fitting to worry if your beams will match each other, or even, dare we say it, the floorboards, or, heaven forbid, *the furniture?*

The answer is yes. It is appropriate, and if you're a homeowner, it will definitely happen; even if you never actually discuss it, it will certainly cross your mind. If you are going so far as to utilize antique materials in the design of your home, you are naturally going to focus on other design-related issues, including color, texture, species, grain pattern, and tone. And if you're using other recycled materials such as brick, chances are you'll be worried that they are uniform in size and color as well.

That said, while it is highly likely that you will concern yourself with the visual characteristics of the materials you use, it is neither probable nor realistic to expect reclaimed materials to exactly match anything: neither the floors nor the walls, nor your couch, nor each other.

Structures put up by our forefathers two hundred years ago were timberframe. They used the trees that were available around their site and did not consider using a particular species for a particular job. Many different kinds of available hardwoods had more than enough strength to go into building a structure, be it a cabin or a barn. Most logging was done with horses or mules, so it was natural for them to use the mix of species indigenous to their particular farm or home site.

If, however, you absolutely *must* have like-toned materials, you will be happy to know that there has been great success with many different stains, waxes, and finishes available for use on reclaimed wood. When working with processed timbers, antique paneling, and especially old flooring, it is very easy to mix complementary stains. The colors simply work together, allowing the timeless beauty of the wood to come through; they also blend areas of the wood that need to be closer to the same shades of color. Another process that is often used to reveal the original colors and grain of wood, including walnut, cherry, chestnut, or mixed oak, is to refine it even further by resawing the timbers. Planing an inch or two along the length of the timber allows the original beauty of the woods to come alive.

> While it is highly likely that you will concern yourself with the visual characteristics of the materials you use, it is neither probable nor realistic to expect reclaimed materials to exactly match anything.

As evidenced here, wood needn't match in color or texture: to the left is a honey-colored reclaimed door of wide-plank pine; the walls, also constructed of reclaimed materials, are blond and more finely finished; and the massive overhead beam is recycled, with its antique rough-hewn qualities completely visible. Photo by Gil Stose.

Photo by Gil Stose.

Visual Characteristics of Reclaimed Timber

There are many irregularities in the natural features of timeworn timber. For example, there are areas where the edge of a tree has a naturally wavy appearance. When this is left on a beam, it is called "the waning effect." People will often see this and say, "It's not perfectly square," or "It's not a complete rectangle, so I don't know whether it will work or not." But in more than 70 percent of all cases, these irregularities appear on some of what we call the highly desirable "feature" beams or "character logs," which have a warm, natural edge with a highly weathered look. They may contain scars, burls, or other aesthetically pleasing **characteristics**. Ultimately, this timeworn appearance has a dramatic effect on clients, particularly when they see the beams in a completed project.

The same is true of antique brick; they were mixed and shaped by hand labor, and the clay used would have had different colors and tones in it, depending on what kinds of material were readily available.

Other characteristics of recycled wood may include the following:

- Stress fractures
- Fossil-insect scarring
- Mortise, nail, or bolt holes
- Natural color variation
- Original hewn markings
- Original end mark, or jobber stamp (much like a cattle brand, this represents the name of the original craftsman)

Refinement and Color

If you ask five different people what colors they like, or what kind of music they prefer, chances are you'll receive five different answers. And likewise, most people prefer different stages of refinement when utilizing antique products in their home. Some may prefer a weathered, raw, unfinished rustic look; others may prefer a "finer" style that actively utilizes color and polish. In their purest form, recycled antique materials are generally a rich gray and brown, containing characteristics that include weathering, checks, cracks, and knotholes. Barn board, for example, may have a quarter-inch recess in the grain, clearly showing many years of weathering by wind, snow, ice, heat, and other elements. Depending on where they were placed in the original structure and how exposed they were to the elements, timber will have different color tones: silver-gray, gray, brown, and brown-gray. It can then be pressure-washed, which prepares the wood for different levels of finishing. Or it might be hand-sanded for a different kind of effect, or even power-sanded for a more refined look. At this stage, stains can be applied to equalize or neutralize the colors that emerge under the years of weathering. But again, no two pieces of wood—no matter how well selected, sanded, or stained—will match *exactly*. Like a human fingerprint, each species and each piece of wood possesses a look all its own.

As we have discussed, one of the enormous benefits of using reclaimed wood—especially antique wood beams—is the historical, *living* connection to the artisanship of the past: the incredible energy and skill of long-ago craftsmen becomes a part of each home into which the material is incorporated. Literally every beam, having been hewn by hand, is different; each has its own characteristics, color, and history. Great care has been taken to make the beam into a structural beam, and living with it is, in fact, a gift of living with something historically significant. Furthermore, because these beams are of such great historical import, visually beautiful, and not always readily obtainable, they have a much greater value than newer wood, ultimately increasing the overall value of the property into which they are placed.

Frequently Asked Questions

As you become increasingly familiar with the properties of reclaimed materials, many questions will undoubtedly arise regarding wood properties, species, flexibility, age, strength, visual characteristics, and much more. It doesn't matter whether you're a seasoned homeowner, builder, architect, or designer; every question is worthy, and should be asked. Here are answers to some of the more frequently asked questions we've encountered:

Do I have to keep all of those little holes in the beams?

Those are old mystery mortise holes; they're statements of the past. They are usually rectangular holes in the wood that have been chiseled out by hand, either partially or all the way, through a beam or column. The hole allows the tenon—which is a piece shaped by hand—to fit into the mortise hole. There should also be a hand-carved peg on the other end to secure the tenon in the hole so that it cannot be unintentionally released. These old mortise holes generally blend into the antique wood like an original design, accentuating the beauty of the wood and highlighting the craftsmanship of the original millwright. There is honesty in showing old mortise and bolt holes, but they can be filled if desired by putting in plugs of similarly colored material, then staining and blending them together so the old holes cannot be seen. However, one could liken this to altering a valuable antique. If mortise holes are left unplugged, it assures future generations that this material has been reused, thus creating a sense of antiquity and design integrity.

What are all those "little chop marks" on the beams? Do they all have to be that texture, or can I have them sanded down to be smoother?

These are varying kinds of "hewing" textures, and are all based on a variety of factors: the tree—its location, density, and age; the tools—the quality of steel used in the ax, broad ax, or adz, and how sharp they were kept; and the cutter—his age, strength, skill, and ability to keep his rhythm. Yes, you can have them sanded down. But again, doing this would be eliminating some of the material's personal character.

What about all those cracks in the boards?

These cracks are part of the beauty of the planks, especially when they're reused for paneling and flooring. They are, for the most part, cured checks that can be pushed together by a skilled installer. They show that the wood is very dry and very stable, which makes this characteristic highly desirable by those who value antiquity as well as quality.

What about the old nail and bolt holes surrounded by blackened areas?

Those are part of the honesty of the look of antique materials. If you don't want the nail and bolt holes in your reclaimed wood, you'll have to pay more in time and money for someone to grade, cut, select, and discard. The result will be wood that has lost its character, history, and dignity.

Color and texture issues are not limited strictly to recycled wood: these antique Chinese pavers range in color from light to dark, their texture from rough to smooth, and their edges from straight to wavy.

Photo by Ed Knapp.

Practical Considerations

As in any potentially costly endeavor involving major changes to your home—whether building a new one from old materials or engaging professionals to do a job that you yourself may not understand in its entirety—it is not only wise but absolutely necessary to approach the task with at least *some* basics in hand. Likewise, if you are a professional builder, architect, designer, or layperson considering a venture into the architectural salvage or recycling business, you'll want to have as much information available to you as possible before you plunge headlong into the professional side of this world. Securing reclaimed materials, choosing them, knowing what you and your clients are going to want and to get *before* an antique structure is demolished—these are all extremely vital phases in the reclamation process.

Finding Reputable Sources of Reclaimed Materials

As noted earlier, a building that is half collapsed or falling in on itself looks like a pile of junk. Most people discover that demolition and salvage work is generally a very dirty, potentially dangerous job with little glory and not much appreciation. But good wood in old structures is

At Vintage Beams & Timbers, hand-hewn timbers show their colors in the afternoon sun; much of the work we do takes place outside. Photo by Susie Adams.

This English Gothic barn serves as head-quarters for Vintage Beams & Timbers. Photos by Susie Adams.

everywhere, and if it has been kept dry and relatively free of bugs, it is very valuable and worth the effort to reclaim it, no matter what it looks like upon first glance. When a demolition and reclamation company considers saving the still-usable parts of a property, many options and possible problems must be considered, including the usual city and county permits, logistics, and especially liability insurance. Also, it must be determined how much of the building and site will be cleaned up, how much of the building is usable, and how much of it may have to be burned if burning is permitted in the existing location. There are safety and EPA rules that must be followed if asbestos or other dangerous substances are present, and very often they are.

If you're an architect, builder, or designer and you're looking for a good source of reclaimed material, check to see how the wood-source companies operate. Many businesses are simply offices with a computer and a warehouse facility.

The broker fills orders from a variety of sources, purchasing from one area or from local people referred to as "pickers," or demolition people. If the broker does not have the material on hand when the order is placed, then the time constraint becomes a major factor in completing a construction job or finding material for a unique or custom order. When using reclaimed lumber products, it is also convenient to go to a reclaimed-wood lumberyard, see the inventory on hand, and select and purchase the product. Always allow ample time to select material, know where it is if not on hand, plan to have it made available, and establish or estimate the approximate time needed so it can be worked into the construction plans of the design and building team.

Design and Supply: A Professional's Approach

A sensible method for designing a new building and getting the most in the way of materials and design plans from a *standing*, ready-for-demolition building is to study the structure in its existing form. This is a very good approach for managing the "design and supply" part of the job. Visualize which elements of the structure will fit into the design of a new home or commercial building, especially one that is currently in the planning stage. "Waste not, want not" is an apt motto for this part of the salvage process. It takes a great deal of forethought to decide how best to dismantle a site to retain its oldest and finest parts.

If you are a salvage company, plan to visit a site or sites where there are at least several structures still standing and have their demolition schedules. What you see will become a good inventory from which clients can compare and then select the types of antique timber suited to their particular needs. It is also critical for architects and designers to know the resources and capabilities of the recycling company supplying materials for their design. Those architects or designers who are experienced in dealing with salvaged wood realize that what will actually work and what is readily available can, unfortunately, be two totally different things. An architect may call and describe a plan with a "needs list" that includes old wood. Total honesty between the architect and supplier will pay off in the long run, resulting in the most successful and satisfying way to do business for all concerned. When the list of materials from the drawing board is compared to what is probable and realistic, common ground is established to satisfy the customer by working out a design that will utilize materials supplied by the sourcing company. It is a challenge for the lumber recycler to come up with a ready-for-demolition, well-constructed building that will

> It takes a great deal of forethought to decide how best to dismantle a site to retain its oldest and finest parts.

A reclaimed circa-1840 log cabin, not far from Vintage Beams, is what the author calls home. Note the local-fieldstone chimney. Photo by Susie Adams.

Practical Considerations

not only meet a special need, but will also be a profitable venture for the company. It takes an experienced eye to make these decisions, so:

- Examine demolition sites and other buildings that have potential, keeping your new design in mind.
- Look at each individual old structure with the new design in mind.
- Consider how to best utilize the materials, columns, or beams.
- Focus on what would produce the best yield, not only from a monetary standpoint but also from a new design standpoint.

It is also essential to consider the preferences of the homeowner and the options and products available when it comes to mixing and matching the various types of reclaimed materials. With all of the sorting, mixing, and matching of different types and pieces of salvaged wood, brick, flooring, and barn board, this can be an overwhelming task. Hand-hewn timbers come in varying sizes and may differ as much as one to three inches from one end of the beam to the other. This has to be considered when allowing for the ends to be properly joined. The same situation comes to light when using the ancient, handmade Chinese bricks that Vintage Beams & Timbers imports. Since they were made in many colors, sizes, and thicknesses by hundreds of different hands, great care must be taken in both blending tones and texture, and installing these products. The time and expense of accomplishing these necessary steps must be addressed at the beginning of a project, so that it doesn't overwhelm builders later on.

The Language of the Business

As a responsible homeowner or professional who is embarking on the reclaiming process, you will undoubtedly be faced with a plethora of new terms and phrases with which you must be familiar. These are a few of the more common terms:

Appliqué beams are timbers that have been kept natural on three sides but sawn flat at the top so they may be attached to a ceiling or wall.

Board foot is a measurement that, singularly, always translates to 1 inch thick, 12 inches long, and 12 inches wide. To find the board foot of your material, multiply its thickness in inches by its width in inches by its length in feet, and divide this figure by 12. This is a cubic measurement that is standard in the lumber industry.

Example: To find the board feet of a piece of lumber 3 inches x 6 inches x 12 feet:
3 inches thick x 6 inches wide x 12 feet long = 216 ÷ 12 = 18 board feet

Circular-sawed lumber is characteristically sawn by a 4- to 5-foot circle-saw blade, which leaves heavy-edged, deep saw marks in the wood.

Floorboards, or floor decking, are very "naily" and are put down on top of the floor joists to hold things in place.

Floor joists are commonly 2 x 8 feet, 10 feet, or 12 feet running parallel to each other and supporting a floor; in turn, they are supported by larger beams, girders, or bearing walls.

Hand-hewn materials have a specific texture that comes as a result of chopping the wood with either a broad ax or an adz.

Pressure-washing antique timber on the Vintage Beams & Timbers property. All the mortise-and-tenon holes and slots are quite visible. Photo by Susie Adams.

Hand-hewn paneling has a "hewn" face that has been sawn from a beam normally 1¹/2 to 2 inches thick.

Metal detection is a critical process, and must take place prior to cutting into old

A close-up example of tried-and-true, mortise-and-tenon joint construction; the joint is held in place by a peg. Photo by Ed Knapp.

beams during the sawing process. A metal detector will show any nails or metal fasteners that may have been left in the wood during its previous use. If this step is not completed, bodily injury is a potential risk.

Mortise is a slot or hole cut into a board, plank, or timber to receive the tenon (or tongue) of another board, plank, or timber. Together they form a joint.

Pegs (also known as wood pegs) were the "nails" of our forefathers. Generally they were hand-carved from harder woods, such as oak and hickory, and used to attach mortise-and-tenon connections. Today, these pegs have been replaced by metal nails, screws, and bolts.

Pit-sawn lumber has been produced by an ancient sawing method in which one man is above the pit and two men are standing in the pit, with a log on a frame suspended over them. A straight, vertical saw mark results from the "push-pull" stroke.

Three pegs keep a massive structural beam in place. Photo by Ed Knapp.

Pressure-washing is a process that will remove all dirt, stones, leaves, and any foreign matter from the wood. A steady stream of water under high pressure leaves salvaged materials clean. Material to be recycled can also be treated in the same manner in order to clean out insects that may have burrowed into the wood over the years. A spray is used during this process that will not only eliminate bugs that might be present, but also prevent any further insects from trying to enter the wood.

Rafter beams come in many different sizes, depending on the architectural design of the structure at hand. Two major types used in timberframing (not including the rafters) are beams (horizontal) and columns (vertical). A true timberframe building will have ceiling girders, joists, and summer beams—an array of timbers with specific designated functions.

Roof boards, or sheeting boards, are used over the rafters, ceiling joists, and other pertinent areas to enclose the roof. They tend to be very "naily" because of the high number of nails needed to hold the roof to the building.

Tenon, a protruding, or "tongue-shaped," carved piece at the end of a wood beam or column that fits into the *mortise* (page 52), which is designed to receive the tenon and make a tight connection; it is then attached with a wooden peg to strengthen the joint. The peg may be hidden, or pegged, all the way through the mortise and tenon. Mystery mortise holes, commonly seen in salvage materials where mortises had a special function at some point in the past, can be plugged with a *mortise plug* or a *mortise patch*. It is a matter of personal preference whether to leave these mortise holes alone or to fill them.

The Wisdom of the Ages

Whether you are a professional or a layperson, as you sift through an unseemly pile of dirty, dusty reclaimed materials with a plan to rebuild or reuse, bear in mind that you are looking at history. Moreover, and perhaps most importantly, you are looking at the kind of design integrity, beauty, and craftsmanship that has endured through the ages. Learn from it; learn from the salvage experts in whom you are putting your trust to secure the strongest, most stable, most unique and individual construction materials— old or new—available.

If you are a layperson, learn something of the material's "personal" history; this will be easier if it's coming from a recently demolished structure or if a dilapidated building has been brought down specifically to secure the materials at hand. If records have been preserved, try to find out who lived there. How old was the structure? Under what conditions was it built? Why was it built? Was it a utilitarian outbuilding such as a barn or was it someone's home? If you are a professional, question your clients on how they plan to live with this material. Are they historically inclined? If not (or even if so), can you shed light for your clients on the artisanship and mastery it took to create these materials for their original owners or inhabitants?

Professional or layperson, homeowner or architect, builder or salvage expert—all those involved in the utilization of reclaimed antique materials are responsible for handing off the baton of design integrity, craftsmanship, and history to the next generation.

Chinking is clearly visible on these reclaimed hand-hewn beams.

Photo by Ed Knapp.

CHAPTER FOUR

The Extended Life of Antique Structures

Over the years, as I have traveled around the country and visited homes and commercial buildings that utilize reclaimed materials, I have come to the realization that the people who are involved in the reclamation process—homeowners, architects, builders, designers, salvage specialists—have a vested interest in the legacy of craftsmanship. They may also, unwittingly, have an interest in the way human history and stories are subtly told by that which makes up someone's physical surroundings.

History percolates beneath the surface of antique materials, be they silver or wood; when they are used for the purpose of home or architectural design, they become an intrinsic part of our day-to-day lives.

Think of your home as a *living* thing, a living cell, and you will come to see that what makes up your home is, likewise, also alive. Have your floorboards been reclaimed from another structure? Was your entire home reconstructed from a building that had been demolished? Was your mantelpiece salvaged from another, long-dilapidated building? What stories can they tell? What is *their* legacy? How will *they* be used 150 years from now?

Throughout this book, you will meet structures both old and new, dilapidated and

Photos by Martha Baskins.

reclaimed. From an old upstate New York railroad depot built eleven years before the start of the Civil War, to a nineteenth-century barn made of solid chestnut boards, to a new home in South Carolina, each structure somehow has a direct connection, a link, to the legacy of another. The materials tell their own stories and pass on their own histories and design integrity, even as they take their place in a new, twenty-first-century home.

The ANDOVER Depot

The Andover Railroad Depot, built in Andover, New York, circa 1851, was one of the last depots on the old Erie Railroad Line. Originally chartered in 1832, the line ran from the banks of the Hudson River to the shores of Lake Erie and was the subject of endless controversy and conflict with the Atlantic and Great Western Railway Companies, among others. Due to age and extreme weather conditions over the years, the Andover Depot became a grave financial concern as well as a liability to the town. The townspeople made a valiant and emotional attempt to raise the necessary funds to restore the building to life as a visitor's center or a museum, but were unable to do so.

As is quite common, the townspeople had a very strong emotional and historical connection to their beloved building, and when it became obvious that they would not be able to save it, they turned to my organization, Vintage Beams & Timbers, Inc. We worked very closely with the town throughout the process of evaluating the structure to see how it might be reclaimed and reused. Ultimately, the people of Andover were delighted to know that their much-loved depot would *not* be destroyed, but rather, resurrected into a home where its integrity, character, and history would remain intact for years to come. Much of the timber from the depot was used in the following home, in Nantahala Gorge, North Carolina. Most of the original dates, stamps, and signatures are still visible on its beams and doors.

The Andover Depot, prior to its demolition. This well-loved, well-used landmark building in small-town upstate New York had a firm place in the hearts of the townspeople, dating back to the 1800s. Fortunately, the building yielded a variety of materials that went into the construction of two homes.

Photo by Susie Adams.

The Nantahala Gorge Home

Locating and dismantling the old Andover Railroad Depot was the first step in constructing this home. After seeing another home built and completed, the owner had some criteria for this one, which we incorporated into a design that used many of the old timbers, doors, and planking from the Andover Depot, as well as antique Chinese brick, which was used extensively in the lower level and arches, walls, floors, and seats of the entry.

The owner was very patient and worked closely with us, giving me a lot of latitude in the overall conceptual design. The home was constructed with a hybrid timberframe, meaning that a timber structure was built, conventional framing was used around it, and antique timber was integrated into it. This method is an excellent alternative for achieving a rustic look while employing modern construction methods. Moreover, it saves quite a bit in the way of resources.

Very often when using reclaimed materials, we find that history reveals itself in the most obvious ways: here, a Mr. Atwood (presumably of Andover, New York) signed his name in charcoal on a beam saved from the Andover Depot; it now supports a second-story loft in the Nantahala Gorge home. While the home has a timber structure, conventional framing was built around it and antique lumber was integrated into it.

Photo by Susie Adams.

Flowers brighten an antique heart-pine sill and set off a restored, colorful antique stained-glass window. Photos by Susie Adams.

The antique stone fireplace, beams, flooring, and bookcase were all rendered from materials culled from the demolition of the Andover Depot.

Not stopping at beams and bricks, the owners of this home insisted on using as many reclaimed materials as they possibly could: here, reclaimed and refinished old hotel doors with restored hardware welcome visitors into nearly every room in the house.

Native fieldstone, a stone mantel, and antique pine flooring were utilized in this walk-around fireplace that opens on one side to the dining room and on the other side to the living room.

The owner of the home in Nantahala Gorge had seen another home built from reclaimed materials. One of the criteria for building his home was that we incorporate materials from the Andover Depot. Here, as well, are reclaimed Chinese bricks, which are used extensively in archways, walls, and seats of entry. Photos by Susie Adams.

The STEIN Barn

In 1992, Earl Stein contacted me about an old barn made of chestnut lumber that had been on his farmstead for more than one hundred years. I found it hard to believe that a barn of the size he described would contain such a great deal of chestnut timber in the planks and siding, so I made arrangements to travel to central Pennsylvania to take a look at it.

Circa 1920, Rhea Stein brings in some of the barn's residents. Photo courtesy of the Stein family.

Earl and his family shared the tales and history about the building of the barn as well as the additional information I needed to make the decision to take on the project. I also spoke with some of the locals and relatives of the Stein family, who lived on the farm in the early 1900s, and they had stories dating back to the late 1800s that would be passed on for generations. As it turned out, a large amount of the barn was American chestnut timber of sound quality. To this day, the American chestnut blight, which killed 3.5 million American chestnuts during the first forty years of the twentieth century, prevents chestnut trees from growing beyond a certain point. At the time when the blight began, most people believed that the only way to stop it was to cut down all the chestnut trees, which is how the Stein barn came to be largely constructed of this beautiful wood.

While I was investigating the Stein barn, a local architect/potential homeowner located in western North Carolina contacted me; he was interested in having a home constructed from the Steins' chestnut timber, if I found it worthy (meaning that it was constructed of quality timber of a certain length that could be dismantled and then reassembled elsewhere), which I did.

Earl Stein was a knowledgeable man and had many different skills, including some background in carpentry and building. He could understand some of my concerns about the logistics of taking his barn down. He and his family were quite accommodating, and we proceeded to work out the logistics for laying out the siding, floorboards, and beams, making the tags, and sketching the existing structure.

With further investigation and research, I began marking the pieces of the barn— timbers, columns, beams—and how they were built; then I photographed, documented and marked each with tags. The barn came down in the middle of the winter and the early spring, was packaged and put onto a truck, and taken to its new southern home.

Massive, time-worn, weathered, well loved and well used, the Stein barn and its out-buildings were largely constructed of chestnut. Photo courtesy of Elaine Godfrey.

Transsoms, Lintels, Mantels, Doors, and Columns: Looking Beyond Flooring and Beams

During the ever-evolving salvage process, when I am well into investigating a building or demolition site's potential, I always take the time to look at each antique structure with a *whole other structure* in mind: how can all the materials, columns, or beams best be utilized? What would be the best yield for a new design? What is the new structure calling for? There are always certain home details that need to be chosen with a great deal of sensitivity. For example, the transom, or lintel, which forms the top beam over the front door of a home, is very significant because a private living space is entered through that door. Transoms are also found over doors in the living room, kitchen, bedrooms, and particularly in family rooms, dens, and recreation rooms. The fireplace mantel is also very close to the heart, as shown by the family heirlooms, photos, and special mementos displayed on it. Selecting the right piece of reclaimed wood—say, an antique beam—for the fireplace mantel can become a very emotional and important decision, especially when future generations are considered.

The Lake Jocassee House

A gentleman had heard of my ventures into salvaging and timberframing and asked if I would be interested in designing and building his timberframe home in the mountains on Lake Jocassee in South Carolina. We specifically spoke about using old timbers in the project, but there would be limitations: the area for this home was very narrow, so its footprint wound up being 50 by 50 feet. At that time, the Stein barn had just been taken down, and much of the timber from the Andover Depot was still available.

The railing and log work of the Stein barn timber, as it was modified and put into

The footprint of the house on Lake Jocassee, South Carolina, was small by any standard: 50 feet by 50 feet, so it was built up several levels rather than out on just one or two. Overlooking the lake, it is a spectacular example of architectural subtlety and intelligent small-house design; the reclaimed timbers it uses allow it to blend in unobtrusively with its surroundings.

Photo by Susie Adams.

Photo by Susie Adams.

New Old House

In a creative nod to historical continuity, these locust handrails were designed in such a way so that guests could personally carve their names into the wood in lieu of signing a guest book. Photos by Susie Adams.

A restored antique porcelain tub is surrounded by reclaimed pine bead-board paneling and heart-pine flooring.

Old-world elegance and practicality: here, antique railroad sinks were converted into bathroom vanities. The mahogany sinks were restored to their original polished splendor, then replumbed for home application.

Nearly unrecognizable in their new home, chestnut timbers from the Stein barn demolition surround the kitchen, juxtaposing a rough-hewn sensibility against modern amenities. The countertops were also made from reclaimed pine.

The desire to use reclaimed and antique materials in one's home extends far beyond that which can be recycled from a barn. Evidence of recycling ingenuity is everywhere in this home, including the telephone stand, which is a salvaged artifact from a long-demolished church.

Built from reclaimed four-inch-thick tree planks, this stairwell is an architectural salvager's dream: the plank treads are clearly visible, and the stairway climbs no less than four stories in this relatively small reclaimed home. Photos by Susie Adams.

Photo by Susie Adams.

New Old House

the completed structure, was very impressive. An overwhelming 75 percent of the materials needed for this new structure were reclaimed from the Stein barn. In addition, the flooring, wall paneling, and all of the standing door and window trim were salvaged from the original Sears & Roebuck building in Chicago.

The demolition of this enormous structure was one of the largest in the country, with many salvage and recycling companies participating in what was a massive effort. The building yielded millions of reusable board feet of pine and oak timbers, and the quality of the wood is reflected in the finished Lake Jocassee home.

Stacks of wood came from the Sears & Roebuck building in Chicago, one of the largets salvage and recycling efforts in the United States. Photo by Ed Knapp.

The Extended Life of the Andover Depot

As I hoped would be the case, the circa-1851 Andover Depot, late of Andover, New York, is alive and well; it's just not in Andover any longer. Half of the wood and timber salvaged from the demolition of this fine old depot went into the western North Carolina home; the other half went to the Lake Jocassee home in South Carolina, which shares space with the timber from Earl Stein's American chestnut barn. Each homeowner lives literally surrounded by the history, the craftsmanship, and the legacy of a beloved structure that was a part of one small town's life for more than one hundred years.

The lake's boathouse was built from the same timber and roofing materials as the main house, and it greatly complements the property. In an ingenious plan, a private hill tram was designed to accommodate guests bringing kayaks from the house down the steep hill to the lakeside.

CHAPTER FIVE

The Mystery and Soul of Reclaimed Materials

The Frog Hollow Home

The Frog Hollow Home is located in Lake Toxaway, North Carolina, and is a magnificent example of how practicality and beauty go hand in hand when designing a home with a wide variety of antique materials, running the gamut from chestnut floorboards reused as doors to Ming Dynasty bricks. The owners did a complete remodel of an existing house that was a very ugly duckling. Their goal was to transform it into the elegant but rustic style of many of the homes and inns in this beautiful vacation spot, and they succeeded brilliantly—right down to the exceptional tree-bark siding, which blends in very well with the surrounding forest.

The original materials for the Lake Toxaway home came from the Lease Barn, near Greenville, Ohio. This structure was approximately 50 feet wide by 100 feet long, and in such dilapidated shape that the owners were going to burn and bury it because of the liability risks it posed. Luckily, we were able to persuade Mrs. Lease to work with us to salvage, reclaim, and ultimately reuse this wonderful timber structure.

Photo by Cameron Krone.

Photo by Gil Stose.

However, the owners of the Lake Toxaway home did not stop at timber: they dedicated themselves to utilizing a wide variety of recycled materials, and the house contains construction materials that hail from not only America, but China and Mexico as well. The flooring is antique oak of random width, and its standing age—how long it has been in use in a structure—is approximately one hundred years old. Its actual age is somewhere around three hundred years old, including the age of the tree plus the standing time in the structure. Antique Chinese brick pavers have been incorporated in the lower-level billiard/game room; they come from Kunming, China, and are approximately two to three hundred years old, dating to the Ming Dynasty. From the lower level up, an old dogwood tree has found service as the base of the stairwell. The structural side of the railing on the top is a mix of wavy dogwood trees, the branches cast from very detailed and ornate wrought iron.

Throughout the house, old chestnut planks were formed and made into rustic doors; all hardware is authentic and antique. The house is an effective blend of old-timber details—what we call tree timbers—as well as old-looking plasterwork and complementary colors that should be credited to the owner and her design team. Eclectic and interesting antique pieces collected by the author from all over the world furnish the home. An Asian flavor emanates from the sitting room off the game room; juxtaposed against the timber detailing, the older materials in this room have a very definite oriental feel to them.

The outside decks and fireplaces offer an external sanctuary from which the owners and their family and friends can enjoy the stunning scenery of the area; these deck spaces are literally outdoor rooms, physically and psychologically extending the warmth and style of the interior structure of the house.

Wide, antique Chinese pavers dating back to the Ming Dynasty were used as flooring in the hall that leads to the family game room. The varying colors and textures complement each other and offset the hand-carved Asian-style doors, which in turn flow into the design of the rest of the room, thanks to baseboards of the same material and color. Photo by Gil Stose.

The doorways at the Lake Toxaway home are sashed with rough-hewn chestnut timbers; note the uneven edges, the knotholes, and, on the far doorframe, the mortise holes. The rusticity of this material is set off by the clean lines of the marble bathroom vanity countertop, as well as the similarly toned bathroom tiles down the hall. A hotel-style towel rack adds elegance to the rustic beauty of the wood and tile.

The owners of the Lake Toxaway home very much wanted to extend the interior of their home to the outdoors; they did this by creating several decks that function as outdoor rooms. This covered deck and indoor/outdoor fireplace look out over the lake. The coffee table is a reclaimed slaughter bench. (Note the antique chicken crate hanging above the left-hand seats.) The chairs and bench provide comfortable rustic-style seating. Photos by Gil Stose.

Reclaimed chestnut kitchen cabinetry and hand-wrought hardware create a sharply contrasting, sturdy base for this antique-style farmhouse sink, which sits on top of it. Black granite countertops were used for a modernizing touch. The dark color provides another point of visual interest, and granite is virtually indestructible, won't stain, and is easy to keep clean. The strategically positioned soft high-hat lighting is recessed into a chestnut beam above the sink; this is another creative way to take advantage of the stability and density of this reclaimed material while providing substantial kitchen lighting. Photos by Gil Stose.

Outside decks and fireplaces are literally outdoor rooms, physically and psychologically extending the rustic warmth and style of the interior structure of the house.

This antique wide-plank dining room table complements a truly original work of art—the freestanding
hutch, a one-of-a-kind piece that provides eye-
catching storage for heirloom antique china. The
wood from which it is constructed is antique, right
down to the bead board; tree bark provides utilitarian accents. Notice the pinecone at the joint on the
lower right-hand underside of the hutch. The bot-
tom shelf railings are also constructed from tree
bark and branches.

The master bedroom suite features hewn timbers
with natural tree edges, surrounded and complemented by rough-textured plaster walls and ceilings, and wrought-iron hardware. The ceiling fan
adds an Asian touch in an unobtrusive manner.
Note the antique wide-plank knotty oak floors.

An antique mirror has been recessed into the wall above the vanity in the guest bathroom, and is highlighted with antique barn-board trim. Photo by Gil Stose.

Old barn board was used as paneling and painted with one coat of white paint to allow the texture of the wood to show through. An antique black wrought-iron sconce adds a touch of elegant simplicity to the rougher texture of the paneling. Photo by Gil Stose.

This Lake Toxaway house and boathouse was architecturally designed to blend seamlessly into the stunning North Carolina scenery that surrounds them. Virtually every type of reclaimed material was utilized in this home, from antique bricks to floorboards to wrought iron. Photo by Cameron Krone.

Attention to detail is evident all over the house. Here, a locust-wood newel post is capped by a custom-made copper top and band to prevent water damage. The nails are also copper. Photo by Gil Stose.

A Contemporary Montana Residence

Featured on the television show *Homes Across America*, this Montana home is an eclectic contemporary blend of prairie timberframing, natural stone, and granite. The result is a home that is organic in feel; the variety of materials utilized in its construction work together in seamless harmony to create a beautiful, elegant, rustic, yet livable warm space. This home used five tractor-trailer loads of products from Vintage Beams & Timbers, Inc., ranging from hewn-siding applications, to bark-edged materials, to wide-plank old floors.

> The variety of materials utilized work together in seamless harmony to create a beautiful, elegant, rustic, yet livable warm space.

Timbers three to four inches thick were applied to the exterior and chinked in a traditional manner to give the home the appearance of a log cabin. The approach from outside shows an expanse that looks like one log cabin attached to another, featuring board-and-batten elements of old barn board. All of the overhangs and decks were predominantly made of old 6 x 6-foot timbers, and 8 x 8-foot timbers were used for some of the roof decking. Upon entering the home, a view of the pergola, or sunroom, displays how the old tree timbers were put to use. The majority of the flooring is made of old wide-plank flooring, mixed with stone. In the foyer, the wood and stone work together, and are curved and shaped to draw the eye downward to this feature. The contemporary kitchen blends stone, timber, wood, and granite, the latter of which is juxtaposed against the warmth of the cabinetry. Ultimately, about to 60 percent of the material used in the remodel of this house was recycled or salvaged.

Facing and overleaf:
The exterior porches and terraces are enhanced by hewn timbers complemented with a log trellis overhead. Timber and natural log structures were incorporated throughout this Montana home. Photo courtesy of Fullerton Architects.

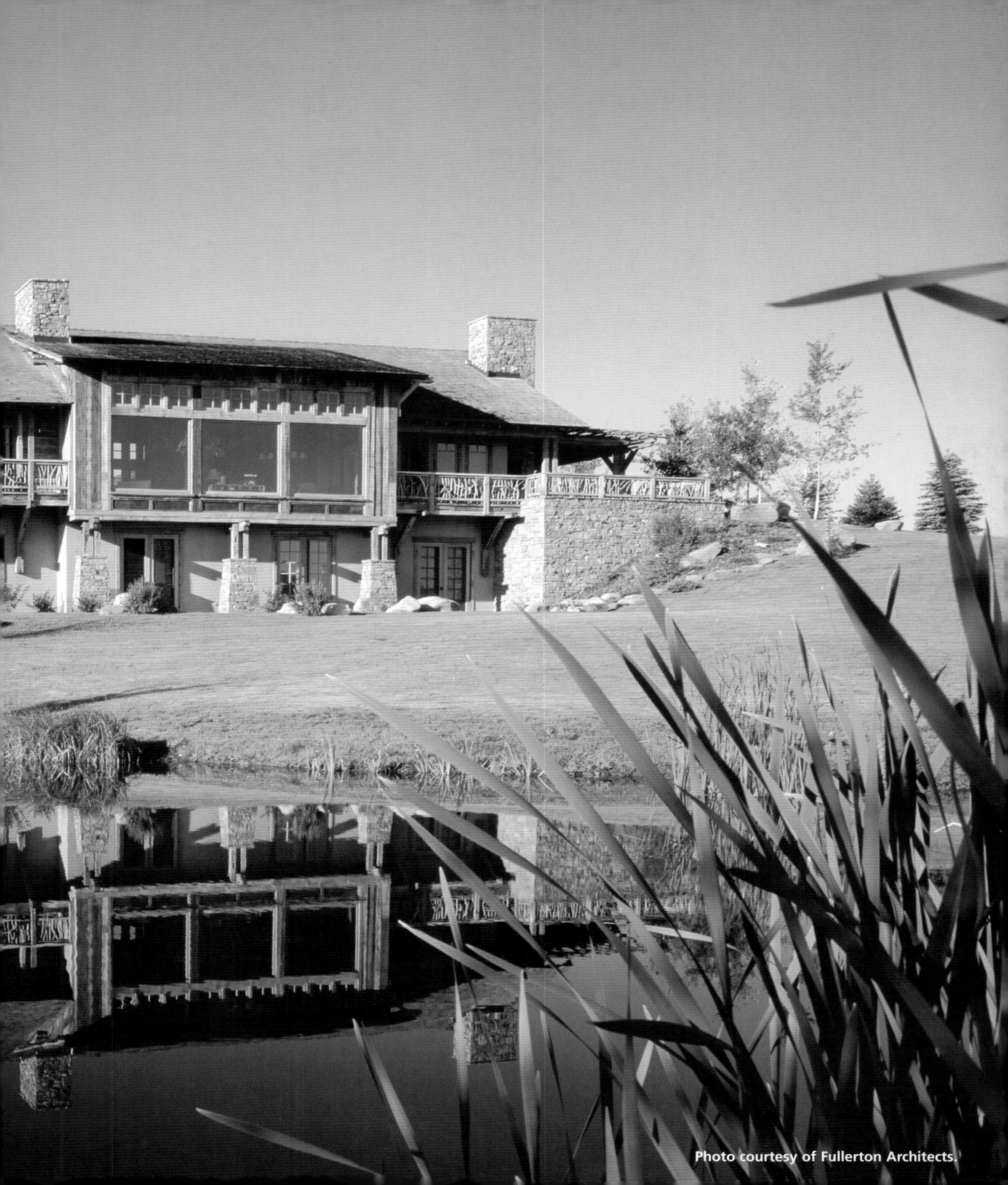

Photo courtesy of Fullerton Architects.

The entry and front doors are covered and flanked by reclaimed beam columns supported by native stone column bases. The entire roof and overhangs utilize hewn timber and roof planking. This home is a wonderful blend of mountain cabin and contemporary design. Photos courtesy of Fullerton Architects.

The Mystery and Soul of Reclaimed Materials

An exterior view of this rustic, nearly palatial Montana home clearly shows its log-plank siding, which runs horizontally below the vertical weathered antique oak siding. This change in the direction of the siding creates a natural *belt-line*, a subtle architectural detail that provides a graceful transition from one part of the exterior to the other. The corner posts and window trim are full-round logs, and the roof is cedar shakes.

This gable-end porch structure is a pleasant setting providing shade and protection for the porches below. Note the irregular ends of beams running horizontal. Ends are left weathered and uneven for natural effects. Branch and tree trims add a nice touch. Photos courtesy of Fullerton Architects.

Photo courtesy of Fullerton Architects.

These comfortable prairie settings reflect warm atmospheres complemented with antique wood and timbers. Photos courtesy of Fullerton Architects.

A striking example of how a wide variety of reclaimed materials of different tones, textures, and colors can successfully work together and complement each other: in this state-of-the-art kitchen, dark antique wide-plank flooring provides a warm base for honey-toned antique-style cabinetry, a white farmhouse sink that flows into matching white countertops, and hewn-beam mantels used throughout the room. Local stone is extensively used, and the pass-through above the countertop range allows additional light to flow through the room. All of the beam ends above the sky-lights were left irregular, and the tenon slots are clearly visible, thus highlighting the mysterious history of the old wood used in this contemporary home. Photos courtesy of Fullerton Architects.

This cozy bedroom and bathroom (right) has the aura of a 200-year-old log cabin. Utilizing hand-hewn floor beams with natural waning and chinking, the wall paneling is truly authentic in design and materials. Ceiling beams in this room and the sun room (right) are approximately 175-year-old antique wood and lumber. Photos courtesy of Fullerton Architects.

The master bedroom ceiling is multifunctional: constructed of highly distressed antique timbers and two-inch-thick floor planks mottled with age, it also serves as the floor of the loft above the bedroom.

Time is not the only element that has added substantial character to these ceiling boards and timbers: if you look closely, you can see a great many (now empty) tenon slots, peg holes, and knots. The age, dryness, and stability of these materials attest to their powerful strength, which is enough to support the floor above them.

The master bath continues the use of heavily distressed antique timbers and reclaimed barn board of different colors and tones. Again, notice the peg holes and tenon slots on the vertical beam running against the wall. The rusticity of this material is in sharp contrast to the polished granite tub setting and white porcelain. Photos courtesy of Fullerton Architects.

Highgate Mountain Home

The Highgate Home is located on the top of a mountain in western North Carolina. An authentically reconstructed log-and-timber home, it makes extensive use of architectural-salvage windows and doors, barn boards, and barn-board trim, giving the feel of a rustic lodge. Several renowned designers were involved in this building project; it is truly a feast for the eyes and senses to behold.

Upon looking at the house from the exterior, it's clear that the owners have gone to great lengths to allow this house and its guesthouse to blend into the site's surroundings. The use of antique beams, native fieldstone, timbers, and logs both inside and outside of the home—even in the kitchen and bathroom—give it a surprisingly formal feel once you step inside. Not limited to American ingenuity, the use of timber framing was extremely popular abroad, particularly in England during the Tudor period; this more classic style is reflected in the beaming of the living room in the main house.

> In this house, the walls are very much details in themselves.

The log walls, now weathered to a silvery gray, are visually dramatic. Generally, walls literally disappear into the background of a space, providing a launching point for details. However, in this house, the walls are very much details in themselves. The log siding is continued in the interior structure of the home and in nearly every room of the house, providing a sense of the ageless and historic wherever you look.

The dovetailed corners in the entry were restored to their original configuration; to their left are reapplied antique shingles. The banister and railing are antique timbers. Upon entering through this door, visitors are greeted by the log walls and weathered timber doorways, which are continued throughout the house. Photo by Gil Stose.

Loosely placed native fieldstone walkways, as well as the warm fragrance of a strategically placed herb garden, welcome visitors to this home. The garden bench, a fine example of traditional rustic furniture at its best, is made of mountain laurel. Note the reclaimed log siding on the exterior of the dormer above and on the rear wall of the house. The cabin adjacent to the main house employs a recycled, rusted tin roof.

More formal in style than the rest of the house and the cabin, the living room combines distinctly Tudor-style beamed plaster walls with local fieldstone for the fireplace. The chandelier, built from twigs and capped off with formal, knife-pleated individual shades, provides subtle lighting and eye-catching rustic detail. Photos by Gil Stose.

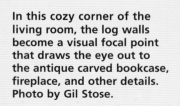

In this cozy corner of the
living room, the log walls
become a visual focal point
that draws the eye out to
the antique carved bookcase,
fireplace, and other details.
Photo by Gil Stose.

106

The juxtaposition of formal and hand-hewn is carried through the house into the kitchen, where Italian-style cabinetry and a marble-topped island sit side by side with the rough-hewn log walls and antique timber posts and baseboard. The flooring of antique wide-plank pine shows its age as well and provides a strong color and textural contrast to the walls and modern woodwork. Photo by Gil Stose.

A traditional formal headboard, nightstand, and mirror blend with the log walls to create a unique kind of home design: formal log style. Photo by Gil Stose.

One of the most visually engaging rooms of the house is the bathroom: the antique log walls were sealed with water repellant. The pine floor was stenciled to provide a shock of color in an otherwise neutral space, then sealed. The basins of these traditional wrought-iron sinks were replaced by handmade bowls; open underneath the fixtures, they provide ample room for storing towels and other necessities. Snake-like wrought-iron sconces add eye-catching detail to the ambience. Photo by Gil Stose.

The back porch of the guesthouse offers a visual mélange of materials, textures, tones, and colors: the roof is rusted red tin, the siding is barn board, the shingles are reclaimed antiques, the porch is supported by local fieldstone pillars, and newel-post railings and pickets are made of antique timber. Photo by Gil Stose.

CHAPTER SIX

Innovative and Artistic Architecture

The Highland Cliff Home

Nestled deep in the Smoky Mountains of western North Carolina, the area surrounding the town of Cashiers lays claim to an abundance of lakefront cottages, vacation homes, and lodges. The raw natural beauty of the place doubtless influences the architecture and design of many of the structures in the area, and the Highland Cliff Home is no different.

At a modest 1,600 square feet, the Highland Cliff Home sits on the edge of a gorge in Cashiers. Prior to the building process, the owner had saved some logs from an old cabin and was hoping to incorporate them into this new site. When she came to me, we discussed what her needs were, and she asked that I design her new home with several things in mind: the old timbers, her budget, several pieces of existing furniture, and her dog, Rags. Ultimately, we designed a home that had many distinctive features, including a redwood shower with glass skylights; a covered porch built from antique lumber, overlooking the gorge; a stairwell in the main room, built from log pieces; salvaged doors gathered from the owner's many travels; a private entrance for Rags, leading into the owner's walk-in closet; and an additional, lockable dog door accessing the rest of the home.

Photo by Gil Stose.

It was decided that the new home would be constructed almost as if it were an integral part of the mountain and the stunning North Carolina landscape; it would be built on the edge of a cliff and would visually flow into the forest tree line. Tall concrete columns were superficially given the appearance of timber, and were connected by several layers of flat sod-grass roofs. Enormous reclaimed timbers from Oregon, used to support the roofs, were really the inspiration for the vast design because of their sheer size and massive length—for example, 12 x 28 x 40 feet long. Timber beams running through the dining room are hand-hewn hemlock, approximately 12 x 18 feet, and were reclaimed from the Jordan barn in western New York. Some of the additional timbers are 12 x 12-foot cherry beams. The floors and cabinetry are constructed of antique barn wood. The

Interior timbers applied to the inside of the finished wallboard give the appearance of structural timber, when, in fact, they are a visual architectural detail. From floor to ceiling, these timbers create a different kind of texture in the space. Photo by Gil Stose.

extensive use of glass on the side of the house overlooking the mountain opens up the house even further, giving it an airy, spacious feeling by bringing in the magnificent outdoors. Moreover, the owner made every attempt to save and use each tree that was cut from the site: the three-story stairwell surrounds one of the site's old oaks, which in turn is used as the support for the spiral stairway, the walls were crafted from sawn shingles, and the treads were made from tree logs. All of the stonework was crafted from local stone.

The result is a livable, comfortable home totally unique in design, which utilizes geometry, light, color, and texture, as well as powerfully strong reclaimed materials.

Even rhododendron handles are reused. Here, they have been applied to barnboard cabinetry. Photo by Gil Stose.

Upon entry, the shingled stairwell begins at the base of the stair treads, which are constructed from reclaimed timbers. The reclaimed rhododendron and tree-log banister winds its way up the stairwell, providing a visual circular contrast to the linear dimensions of the mammoth horizontal beam to the left and the stair treads.

The focus of the stairwell is the tree in the center, which supports the log treads. The ceiling is constructed of copper and is accented by domed skylighting. The eye-catching side walls of the stairwell are wavy shingles. Photos by Gil Stose.

The upstairs balcony is entirely constructed of timber. Overlooking the
great room, it is accessed from behind
the fireplace through the study, and is
supported by one of the trees that
was salvaged from the construction
site. The strength of these salvaged
trees combined with the enormous
timbers that comprise the structural
base for the balcony are a testament
to the stability of recycled wood.
Photo by Gil Stose.

One of the old log cabin beams that the owner had saved is now being used as the fireplace mantel, set atop native-fieldstone surround. Photo by Gil Stose.

In an attempt to use every kind of reclaimed timber we could find in this project, we employed short pieces and ends of logs as stairwell treads. The flooring was comprised of old yellow-pine floorboards. The large beams carrying the upper loft were brought in from a barn to supplement the existing log cabin timber that the owner had saved, and the structural beams in the ceiling came from the original log cabin. A hybrid of new framing methods and traditional timberframing, this design was successful in maintaining the owner's budget and creating the aesthetic mountain atmosphere the owner was trying to achieve. Photo by Gil Stose.

The powder room is a textural feast for the eyes; here, distressed green tiles surround a sink that is supported on one side by reclaimed tree timber. The bathroom door is reclaimed barn wood, and a massive hand-hewn beam gives the impression of physically holding the entire room together. Photos by Gil Stose.

Pegs, notching, barnboard cabinetry, and thick wood-plank countertops are a testament to the long-lasting stability, design integrity, and beauty of reclaimed wood.

The Hemingway House

Characteristic Creativity Using Reclaimed Materials

While visiting the Key West home of legendary author Ernest Hemingway, it is very easy to see what an eccentric, creative, artistic character he was. A man who liked his whiskey regularly and in large quantities, Hemingway lived there during Prohibition; this, of course, led to some level of involvement in smuggling, along with a variety of other adventures.

In addition to imbibing, Hemingway was also an ardent fan of history, salvage, and tradition, and he spent many hours relaxing and unwinding at a local tavern, Sloppy Joe's, which is still in existence. The tavern was undergoing a moving/remodeling project, and one of the items that was to be discarded was the urinal from the men's room. During the remodeling process it was removed and left outside the tavern to be thrown away. Hemingway was a bit upset when he discovered it there, and inquired of the owner why his favorite urinal was sitting out in the street.

"I put a lot of money down that drain," Hemingway said, and promptly proceeded to make other plans for it.

Hemingway's wife at the time was extremely meticulous about the care of the grounds around the house they shared. She had a huge swimming pool built for an exorbitant sum of money—the first swimming pool in the Keys—and Papa (as he was known) wasn't particularly thrilled with the price of the project. He decided to take the urinal from Sloppy Joe's and place it in the garden for his many cats to use as a cat fountain, thus making good use of this discarded object. His wife, of course, was less than pleased, but Papa responded in no uncertain terms: "Either make the cat fountain work, or the pool goes." So Mrs. Hemingway placed the urinal in a prominent position in the courtyard at the front of the pool, surrounded it with hand-painted French tiles, and planted native plants and flowers behind it. An exquisite old Italian urn holds a pump and the water flows out of it, giving the urn a beautiful discoloration. At first look, the old urinal from Sloppy Joe's Tavern is a stunning European lavabo and could probably be considered one of the very first recycling projects in America. It's still proudly in use today by the great-great-grandcats of those belonging to Papa and Mrs. Hemingway. Photo by Ed Knapp.

CHAPTER SEVEN

The Elegant Side of Rustic

Throughout this book, we have examined the use of reclaimed and recycled materials in a variety of building scenarios: entire structures are taken down, moved from one site to another, rebuilt, and restored; beams from the original, dilapidated nineteenth-century Andover Depot are reused in three different new homes; what might be construed as an ordinary way to get from one floor to another—the ubiquitous stairwell—emerges in a North Carolina home as a work of modernized rustic art in and of itself. All of these sites bear one unifying theme: they all carry on a tradition of design integrity and craftsmanship well into the future.

Largely, these sites have all been somewhat traditional, rustic-style country homes. But what of the more formal elegant homes that match rustic resources with refined local materials? The houses that we are going to visit in the upcoming pages take the idea of utilizing reclaimed materials one step further: they blend the hand-hewn rawness and design integrity of days gone by with modern lines, textures, and surroundings to produce something truly unique, functional, beautiful, and elegant.

The exterior of the Gold Tree Cottage shows how reclaimed timbers, glass, and extreme geometry can be used to create dazzling visual effects. This home is a timber structure, approximately four stories tall (including the foundation base). The texture of the roofing materials (cedar shakes) and the walls (also cedar shingles) softens the hard roof lines. Photo by Gil Stose.

The Gold Tree Cottage

Drawing from a modern-influenced architectural aesthetic, architect Jim Fox planned his design around an established house. The new owners elaborated on the interior and the details, removing carpet and incorporating antique lumber and western furnishings, which altered the mood of the entire home. Finished with recycled and reclaimed materials, most of the timber elements are weathered gray pieces that contrast with the antique wide-plank oak flooring; they also complement the American and Indonesian old-world antiques. Old plank doors are juxtaposed against modern architectural lines created by glass placed at 45-degree angles.

Literally built out of the side of the mountain and cantilevered in several different directions, the Gold Tree Cottage offers visitors breathtaking views, along with a sense of hovering above the ground while strolling on the deck.

Wide antique oak flooring complements this cozy living room fireplace, built from native fieldstone. Photo by Gil Stose.

This bedroom appears to be floating over the treetops. In a part of the house that is cantilevered over the ground, the bedroom window gives the illusion of being one piece, even though its mitered corners are joined. Photo by Gil Stose.

The Elegant Side of Rustic

125

The House at Lake Burton

The old water-powered Millmont Grist Mill, circa 1840, was the hub of all trade and farm activity in the township of Millmont, Pennsylvania. Farmers brought their crops and goods to be milled, paying the mill owners with a portion of their milled goods in lieu of monetary recompense. The mill was five stories tall, approximately 100 feet wide and 300 feet long, and the timbers were all of red and white oak. In true recycled form, this incredible structure—steeped in history—was transformed into a beautiful home. All of the large structural oak timbers were installed in the lower level of the main house and many were placed back into their original fits and joinery. Original oak was used in the ceilings of both the interior and exterior areas of the home. The master bedroom has a trellis system built from white birch that was harvested from standing dead timber in the Adirondacks. The great room has a nautical theme, with timber trusses made of resawn pine timber and numerous carved corbels and braces; the balcony is carved from cherry. Distressed and reclaimed cherry is used extensively throughout the living room, dining room, stairwells, and hallways, and some of the bedrooms were appointed with antique log siding and chestnut flooring.

The exterior of this home, as viewed from the lake, is an example of country elegance, clearly showing how antique lumber creates authenticity by blending with the abundant local stone, the gambrel roof design, and Palladian doors and windows. Photos courtesy of Harrison Design Associates, Inc.

Another example of the ability to transcend rustic materials for a more elegant old-world feel is seen in this river-rock fireplace with its antique timber mantel. The timber truss above is made of antique pine and traditional joinery. The finials and curved beam ends were all made by Vintage Beams & Timbers. Photo by Gil Stose.

The dining room table at the Gold Tree Cottage is made from an antique plank door. Notice the contrasting reclaimed ceiling beams and the fieldstone kitchen hearth into which the commercial range top and hood are recessed.

The owners of this home have made excellent use of both built-in modern convenience and hand-hewn cabinetry; on the far side of the kitchen is a small wine cooler underneath the cabinetry, alongside a wet sink. Photo by Gil Stose.

Antique floor timbers were sawn in half and applied to the walls of one of the children's bedrooms, creating the look of an authentic cabin. The chinking is a light gray color, and the floors and trim are antique chestnut lumber. Photo by Gil Stose.

The master bedroom features a unique, white birch tree trellis set off by grey paneling. The storm-damaged trees, approximately five years dead and still standing in the forest, were hand-logged. All parts of the trees were utilized in this design. Photo by Gil Stose.

The game room in the lower level of the main house has ceiling beams, columns, and curved brackets—all original materials reclaimed from the old Millmont Grist Mill. The owners agreed to design the room around the existing structure; for example, ceiling joists went back into the original mortise pockets of the girt beams, making the restored room feel very authentic. The oak column is a structural detail, supporting the second story. Even the pool table is hand-hewn. Photo by Gil Stose.

The covered porch is enhanced by exposed hand-hewn timber, reclaimed from the Barker barn in Ohio. The timber was pressure-washed and sealed with a clear finish. Notice the exposed mortise holes. Local stone was used on the floor and the arches. Photo by Gil Stose.

Color variations, knots, old nail holes, checks, and cracks lend personality and a sense of history to this children's checker table and chairs, built from antique lumber. Photo by Gil Stose.

"God is in the details." The architect Mies van der Rohe was right: the base of this cherry column is surrounded by a cherry border, which complements the stone tile. The tile, corbel, and column do not compete with the stone; instead, the textures and colors flow seamlessly into each other. Photo by Ed Knapp.

Opposite:
Seen from the main house, the boathouse features a similar gambrel roof line and a terraced walk that is cantilevered over the water. The lower floor was constructed at water level and is used for storage; the two upper levels serve as a studio and guest accommodations. Photo courtesy of Harrison Design Associates, Inc.

A Tuscan Villa in Atlanta

Montepulciano? Rapalano Terme? Montereggioni? Florence? Atlanta. (Yes, Atlanta.) This home, built true to the Tuscan Villa style with Palladian influences, was designed by Harrison Design & Associates, with Vintage Beams & Timbers, Inc. A fine example of a home whose old timber, honesty, and integrity of design are intact but have been complemented by different elements from around the world, this villa is elegant but well-balanced, marrying the traditional to the contemporary.

Italian stone floors blend with antique oak flooring reclaimed from an Ohio barn. The veranda ceiling is paneled with sawn antique oak timbers, while other ceilings throughout the house have arched oak beams between them, giving the illusion of a higher ceiling. The old timbers in the kitchen are hand-hewn in their natural form; the mortise holes and notches are quite visible. Wide-plank floors throughout were installed and stained in place to pull out the color variations of the wood doors and woodwork. A guest cottage situated at the back of the home is surrounded by beautiful flower gardens.

Designed with an authentic Tuscan villa in mind, this Atlanta home is a showcase of tradition, Italian country style, and southern comfort. A veritable mosaic of textures and hand-hewn materials, the villa is as authentic as any seen in the Tuscan countryside, right down to the majestic doorway. The circular courtyard serves as an eye-catching entrance to the main house. Photo courtesy of Harrison Design Associates, Inc.

Hand-hewn beams in these
ceilings are from Pennsylvania.
The flooring (left) is reclaimed
antique Italian floor tile. Photos
courtesy of Harrison Design
Associates, Inc.

Situated in close proximity to the
villa is its equally-authentic stone
guest cottage. The gardens and
loosely laid stone paths over-
grown with flowers and herbs
lead visitors to a remarkable
view. Photos courtesy of Harrison
Design Associates, Inc.

Commercial Applications

Utilizing vintage materials in commercial construction is a growing trend both in the United States and in other countries. Many companies have strived to do so in order to respect our national resources, others because it fits aesthetically with their company's mission statements and atmosphere. From homes across the world and outdoor shops and custom shipbuilding to a café in China, the results are all the same—natural beauty and application of unique architectural elements that create a wonderful ambience.

Bass Pro Outdoor World

Over the years Bass Pro Shops has made a strong effort to work with as many recycled and salvaged materials as possible. In this Charlotte, North Carolina, store, the entry to the lodge makes you feel at home: walls, floors, and ceilings make extensive use of timbers, hand-hewn wallboards, and reclaimed flooring. Throughout the store, the retail display racks are made of old barnboard, rusty tin roofing, old hardware, and nautical antiques. Many building materials that would have otherwise been burned or ended up in the landfill now have a new life.

Seven Foxes Mountain Cabins

Seven Foxes is nestled in the mountains of western North Carolina close to Lake Toxaway. This beautiful resort area has made a valiant attempt to use as much recycled and traditional salvaged furnishings as possible, much to the delight of its many visitors. Vintage materials like corrugated metal, old doors, and vintage walnut, oak, and poplar timbers create a unique down-home retreat.

Jarrett Bay Custom Shipbuilding

Custom shipbuilding is an art and craft all its own, and the folks at Jarrett Bay are some of the best in the business. Antique reclaimed teak lumber is difficult to find and expensive. The craftsmen at Jarrett Bay appreciate the wood and waste very little in their design and applications.

Opposite: Mountain cabins are nestled beyond the entrance to the Seven Foxes, located in the scenic mountains of western North Carolina near Lake Toxaway. They are secluded and well-appointed with many antique and recycled furnishings.

One of the guest bedrooms in this cabin is called Bear Cave. The walls are covered with reclaimed roofing tin, which was cleaned, then sealed. The wainscoting on the walls is from mixed species of antique lumber, such as walnut, oak, and poplar. Note the use of the old trailer door, showing that anything is possible, whimsical, and authentic when using old materials. Photos by Susie Adams.

The Swag

The Swag, a resort-hotel retreat, is located in a most unusual setting in western North Carolina right outside of Maggie Valley. About twenty years ago, the owners bought the top of a mountain and constructed a beautiful, picturesque retreat. The property borders a national forest and the grounds are kept natural. The resulting cabins are all very old with new additions that have been constructed with older materials that make them appear to have been there for several hundred years. The philosophy of the retreat is to provide down-home mountain quiet time with good eating, nice hospitality, and a beautiful setting. People come from near and far to spend time on top of the mountain.

The interior lodge walls of The Swag Mountain Retreat feature antique timber trusses, a coffee table made from a huge African drum, and a chandelier made from discarded antlers.

Opposite: Many antique timbers were also used in exterior construction. Photos by Gil Stose.

Sixty percent of the wood used in this bedroom suite is antique or recycled lumber. The ceiling is antique wide-plank oak; the timber trusses are a mixed species of wood, pressure-washed and left natural with their brown to golden tones. Note that the mortise holes, checks, cracks, and nail holes are all exposed and beautiful. The fireplace is native stone, the flooring is antique country plank flooring (extra wide material), with minimal sanding and three coats of finish. Photo by Gil Stose.

This charming guest log cabin is a great example of how traditional timbers and construction can stand the test of time. Photo by Gil Stose.

Recycled Materials in China

For the last seven years, Vintage Beams & Timbers, Inc., has been working closely with the government and companies in Kunming, China, to promote international trade. The Antique Department of Kunming, along with exporting companies, has been instrumental in developing mutual exchanges of antique and recycled products. Some of these products have been brought into the United States and used over the years, such as old doors, gliding doors, and closet doors with carvings so exquisite that they are often used on a wall or for openings created with just a backdrop of light. America and China are eager to exchange ideas and try to understand traditions, people's ways of life, architectural techniques, and methods of construction.

In China the desire for information from the West is very great. The Chinese want to obtain good, dependable information about the history of the United States that answers the following questions: Who has been building the country, designing the architecture, and shaping the children's lives? What elements contributed to this lifestyle?

The Bluebird Café

The Bluebird Café is an old converted residence in the fast-growing city of Kunming, China, which is slowly losing its traditions to more modern, culturally Western ideas. However, the city still has a rich tradition that includes minority ethnic groups, trading, crafting, and farming. It is also famous for flowers, making it a very colorful city. But in its quest to become an international modern city, many of the older elements are disappearing. Ran Ching, who owns the Bluebird Café, is doing a fine job of saving the old building, exposing the hewn timbers, maintaining the flow of the old home and courtyard, and building a very fun "hot spot" for many local and Western visitors. The theme of the Bluebird Café centers around the courtyard, which is surrounded by the adjoining rooms and kitchens in the traditional Chinese home style.

Built during the Ching Dynasty, the home includes beautiful water features within the courtyard settings and gardens, as well as colorful plaster walls and old Chinese

The view of this quaint courtyard at the Bluebird Café is accentuated by one-hundred-year-old roof tiles. Photo by Yang Hong Chuan.

doors and windows. One of the most interesting artifacts is the old clay-brick tile roof with grass growing through the tiles; it shelters the pizza kitchen area, which services the outside terrace decks. The character of the Bluebird Café is a stark contrast to the high, contemporary buildings that surround it.

The design of the original structure was kept so that the rooms were not extensively affected, but the ceilings were opened to expose the old wood. Every attempt was made to preserve the barrel tile roofs so that as guests look out from the rooms down to the roofs, they can experience the feeling of traditional China. The floors around the terrace and surrounding brick walls have also been kept intact. The café is successful in blending the traditional with the new and it is a treat for international guests as well as the locals.

The entrance gateway to the Bluebird Café echoes the craftsmanship of traditional China. Photo by Yang Hong Chuan.

Resources

Vintage Beams & Timbers, Inc.

P.O. Box 548

Sylva, NC 28779

828.586.0755

828.586.4647 fax

info@vintagebeamsandtimbers.com

www.vintagebeamsandtimbers.com

Vintage Beams & Timbers, Inc. is a multifaceted company that has been a supplier of fine recycled and antique lumber in the United States for over ten years. We pride ourselves on the comprehensive service that we are able to provide our clients. In addition to supplying antique beam material, we also offer custom truss package fabrication, decorative corbel ends, and floorings and paneling materials in a variety of species. Custom sawing of material is available as we have a sawmill on site. We also work closely with a structural engineer if that is a requirement for a particular project.

Vintage Beams & Timbers has a long-standing history of personal service on projects with architects, builders, and homeowners to ensure that the end result of a project is exactly what the homeowner has in mind. For those who appreciate the look of antique timber but are unsure of how to utilize it in your environment, Vintage Beams also offers design service and creative advice on how to employ the materials to fit your personal style and needs.

While we are based in an idyllic farm setting in the mountains of North Carolina, Vintage Beams & Timbers has an international base of operations for both our antiques and our architectural salvage work, with a particular emphasis on reclamation in China. Three-hundred-year-old brick pavers from the Yunnan Province of China are a staple of our operation, providing a beautiful flooring that has an incredible history to be enjoyed now and shared with future generations. A recent expansion of our timber products includes teak timbers and flooring materials, also from China. Further expansion in the realms of exotic antique materials is planned over the next several years, so stay tuned for updates on exciting new materials and products from Vintage Beams & Timbers. Price quotes and proposals for timber packages are available upon request.

Architects, Designers, & Contractors

Norman Askins P.C.

2995 Lookout Place

Atlanta, GA 30305

404.233.6565

Faure Halvorsen Architects

(formerly Fullerton Architects)

122 S. Wilson Avenue

Bozeman, MT 59715

406.587.1204

Harrison Design Associates

3198 Cains Hillo Place, Suite 200

Atlanta, GA 30305

404.365.7760

Bruce Johnson AIA

66 Forest Road

Asheville, NC 28803

828.274.3922

Kronenberger & Sons Restoration

80 E. Main Street

Middletown, CT 06457

800.255.0089 toll-free

860.347.4600 local

860.343.0309 fax

www.kronenbergersons.com

Leatherwood, Inc.
7106 Black Pine Road
Fairview, TN 37062
615.799.1638
615.799.1430 fax

Red Suspenders Timber Frames
4418 CR 256
Nacogdoches, TX 75965
936.564.9465
936.564.6001 fax
info@redsuspenderstf.com
www.redsuspenderstf.com

Yong Pak & Associates, LLC
Attention: Yong Pak
3195 Paces Ferry Place
Atlanta, GA 30305
404.231.3195

Architectural Salvage

Adkins Architectural Antiques
3515 Fannin Street
Houston, TX 77004
800.522.6547 toll-free
713.522.6547
adkins@adkinsantiques.com
www.adkinsantiques.com

Architectural Antiques Warehouse
17985 Highway 27 (at Route 34)
Fairhope, AL 36532
251.928.2880
www.architectural-antiques.com

Architectural Antiquities
Harborside, ME 04642
207.326.4938
www.archantiquities.com

Architectural Salvage
614–618 E. Broadway
Louisville, KY 40202
502.589.0670

Architectural Salvage, Inc.
3 Mill Street
Exeter, NH 03833
603.773.5635
www.oldhousesalvage.com

Asheville Architectural Salvage & Antiques
23 Rankin Avenue
Asheville, NC 28801
828.281.2600

Black Dog Salvage Architectural Antiques & Salvage
1809 B Franklin Road SW
Roanoke, VA 24014
540.343.6200
www.blackdogsalvage.com

The Brass Knob
2311 18th Street NW
Washington, DC 20009
202.332.3370
202.332.5594 fax
bk@thebrassknob.com
www.thebrassknob.com

Caldwell's Building Salvage Resource
195 Bayshore Boulevard
San Francisco, CA 94124
415.550.6777
415.550.0349 fax
www.caldwell-bldg-salvage.com

Carolina Architectural Salvage
See Cogan's Antiques

Cogan's Antiques
110 S. Palmer Street
Ridgeway, SC 29130
803.337.3939
john@cogansantiques.com
www.cogansantiques.com

Greene's Building Supply & Salvage
860 Riverside Drive
Asheville, NC 28804
828.255.0325

Historic Home Supply
213–215 River Street
Troy, NY 12180-3809
518.266.0675

Historic Lumber
519.853.0008
allan@historiclumber.ca
www.historiclumber.ca

Historic Tile Company European Reclamation
4524 Brazil Street
Los Angeles, CA 90039
818.241.2152
818.547.2734 fax
www.historictile.com

Nor'East Architectural Antiques
5 Market Square
Amesbury, MA 01913
978.834.9088
978.834.9089 fax
mail@noreast1.com
www.noreast1.com

Ohmega Salvage
2407 San Pablo Avenue
Berkeley, CA 94703
510.843.7368
510.843.7123 fax
mail@ohmegasalvage.com
www.ohmegasalvage.com

Old House Parts
24 Blue Wave Mall
Kennebunk, ME 04043
207.985.1999
restoration@oldhouseparts.com
www.oldhouseparts.com

Olde Good Things
Main store:
124 West 24th Street
New York, NY 10011
212.989.8401
888.551.7333

400 Atlantic Avenue
Brooklyn, NY 11217
718.935.9742

Warehouse:
450 Gilligan Street
Scranton, PA 18508
570.341.7668
888.233.9678

Online store:
www.ogtstore.com

Portland Architectural Salvage
919 Congress Street
Portland, ME 04101
207.780.0634
www.portlandsalvage.com

Recycling the Past
381 N. Main Street
Barnegat, NJ 08005
609.660.9790
www.recyclingthepast.com

Rejuvenation Hardware
1100 SE Grand Avenue
Portland, OR 97214
503.238.1900

The Salvage Barn
1147 Riverside Drive
Iowa City, IA 52240
319.351.1875

Salvage One
1840 W. Hubbard
Chicago, IL 60622
312.733.0098
www.salvageone.com

Salvage Sale, Inc.
www.salvagesale.com

Seattle Building Salvage
330 Westlake Avenue N
Seattle, WA 98109
206.381.3453

2114 Hewitt Avenue
Everett, WA 98201
425.783.0529
www.seattlebuildingsalvage.com

The Summer Beam Company
21034 Tramp Harbor Road SW
Vashon Island, WA 98070
206.779.4186
thesummerbeam@mindspring.com
www.thesummerbeam.com

Tim & Avi's Salvage Store
2442 N. Central
Indianapolis, IN 46202
317.925.6071
www.architecturalantiques.net

Vermont Salvage Exchange
P.O. Box 453
White River Junction, VT 05001
802.295.7616

2 Lumber Lane
Manchester, NH 03102
603.624.0868
www.vermontsalvage.com

Whole House Building Supply & Salvage
1955 Pulgas Road East
Palo Alto, CA 94303
650.328.8731 warehouse
650.856.0634 office
www.driftwoodsalvage.com

Reclaimed Lumber

Albany Woodworks
P.O. Box 729
Albany, LA 70711
800.551.1282
www.albanywoodworks.com

America Heart Woods
5089 Covington Pike
Arlington, TN 38002
800.554.5765 toll-free
901.382.0577 local
901.386.9593 fax
info@americaheartwoods.com
www.americaheartpine.com

Carlisle Restoration Lumber
1676 Route 9
Stoddard, NH 03464
800.595.9663 toll-free
603.446.3937 local
603.446.3540 fax

1445 Market Street, Suite 100
Denver, CO 80202
866.595.9663 toll-free
303.893.3937 local
303.893.3939 fax
www.wideplankflooring.com

Centre Mills Antique Floors
P.O. Box 16
Aspers, PA 17304
717.334.0249
717.334.6223 fax
www.igateway.com/mall/
homeimp/wood/index.htm

Chestnut Specialists, Inc.
Plymouth, CT
860.283.4209 phone/fax
chestnutspec@aol.com
www.chestnutspec.com

Chestnut Woodworking & Antique Flooring
P.O. Box 204
West Cornwall, CT 06796
860.672.4300
860.672.2441 fax
www.chestnutwoodworking.com

Country Road Associates, Ltd.
63 Front Street
Millbrook, NY 12545
845.677.6041
845.677.6532 fax
www.countryroadassociates.com

Duluth Timber Co.
P.O. Box 16717
Duluth, MN 55816
218.727.2145
218.727.0393 fax
www.duluthtimber.com

Goodwin Heart Pine Company
106 SW 109th Place
Micanopy, FL 32667-9442
800.336.3118 toll-free
352.466.0339 local
352.466.0608 fax
goodwin@heartpine.com
www.heartpine.com

Hill Country Woodworks
507 E. Jackson Street
Burnet, TX 78611
512.756.6950
512.756.2804 fax
www.precisionwoodworks.com

Jefferson Recycled Woodworks
P.O. Box 696
McCloud, CA 96057
530.964.2740
www.ecowood.com

Longleaf Lumber
70 Webster Avenue
Somerville, MA 02143
617.625.3659
617.625.3615 fax
www.longleaflumber.com

Mountain Lumber Company
P.O. Box 289
Ruckersville, VA 22968
804.985.3646
804.985.4105 fax
www.mountainlumber.com

Pinetree Builders
814 SE 23rd Street
Fort Lauderdale, FL 33316
800.383.5598 toll-free
954.760.5800 local
954.760.5833 fax
www.pinetreebuilders.com

Pioneer Millworks
1180 Commercial Drive
Farmington, NY 14425
800.951.9663 toll-free
716.924.9970 local
716.924.9962 fax
www.pioneermillworks.com

Stockton Hardwoods Ltd.
624 Holly Hills Boulevard
St. Louis, MO 63111
800.788.4828
www.heartwoods.com

Timeless Material Company
305 Northfield Drive East
Waterloo, ON N2V 2N4
Canada
800.609.9633
519.883.4016 fax
info@timelessmaterials.com
www.timelessmaterials.com

T. P. Higgins Co.
P.O. Box 772
Prairieville, LA 70769
225.695.6006 phone/fax
www.eantiquewood.com

**West Lincoln Barnboard
& Beams Ltd.**
Rural Route 1
Smithville, ON L0R 2A0
Canada
800.719.9051
905.643.8878
905.643.9219 fax
www.antiquewoods.com

The Woods Company
5045 Kansas Avenue
Chambersburg, PA 17201
888.548.7609 toll-free
717.263.6524 local
717.263.9346 fax
www.thewoodscompany.com

Reclaimed Structures

The Barn People
2218 U.S. Route 5
Windsor, VT 05089
802.674.5898
802.674.6310 fax
barnman@thebarnpeople.com
www.thebarnpeople.com

Cabin & Timber
835 E. Pattison Street
Ely, MN 55731
218.365.6609
218.365.3142 fax
www.cabintimber.com

Chestnut Oak Company
3810 Old Mountain Road
West Suffield, CT 06093-2125
860.668.0382 phone/fax
info@chestnutoakcompany.com
www.chestnutoakcompany.com

Timber & Stone Restorations
5431 E. U.S. Highway 290
Fredericksburg, TX 78624
800.847.2944
830.997.1195 fax
www.timberandstone.com

Antique & Recycled Cabinetry

Louistine Antique Cabinetry
613.526.1001 phone/fax
loucab@magma.ca
www.magma.ca/~loucab/

Olde World Cabinetry
303.736.4378
sales@antiquemantles.com
www.antiquemantles.com

Shibui
215B E. Palace Avenue
Santa Fe, NM 87501
888.TANSU.49
505.986.1117
shibui@shibuihome.com
www.shibuihome.com

Antique & Recycled Fixtures

**Antique Doorknob
Collectors of America**
www.antiquedoorknobs.org

Phyllis Kennedy Hardware
10655 Andrade Drive
Zionsville, IN 46077
317.873.1316
317.873.8662 fax
philken@kennedyhardware.com
www.kennedyhardware.com

Antique & Recycled Lighting

The Antique Lamp Co.
1213 Hertel Avenue
Buffalo, NY 14216
716.871.0508
www.antiquelampco.com

City Lights Antique Lighting
2226 Massachusetts Avenue
Cambridge, MA 02140
617.547.1490
617.497.2074 fax
lights@citylights.nu
citylights.nu

Nesle Inc.
151 E. 57th Street
New York, NY 10022
212.755.0515
212.644.2583 fax
nesle@earthlink.net
www.dir-dd.com/nesle.html

19th Century Lighting Co.
601 N. Broadway Street
Union City, MI 49094
800.34.VILLA
517.741.7383
517.741.4002 fax
lampman@19thcenturylighting.com
19thcenturylighting.com

Vintage Lighting
Peterborough, ON K9J 2A6
Canada
705.742.8078
vintagelighting@vintagelighting.com
www.vintagelighting.com

Antique & Recycled Tile

Antique Articles
1 Hilltop Road
Billerica, MA 01862-9998
978.663.8083
978.663.8083 fax
artiles@earthlink.net
www.antiquearticles.com

The Roof Tile and Slate Company
1209 Carroll Street
Carrollton, TX 75006
800.446.0220
972.242.1923 fax
www.claytile.com

Solar Antique Tiles
306 E. 61st Street
New York, NY 10021
212.755.2403
212.980.2649 fax
pleitao@aol.com
www.solarantiquetiles.com

Tile Antiques
P.O. Box 4505
Seattle, WA 98104
206.632.9675

The Tile Man Inc.
520 Vaiden Road
Louisburg, NC 27549-9638
919.853.6923
919.853.6634 fax
info@thetileman.com
www.thetileman.com

Antique & Recycled Windows & Glass

Fairview Glass
5607 Old National Pike
Frederick, MD 21702
301.371.6783
fairviewgl@aol.com
www.fwp.net/fairviewglass